Strictly BLACKPOOL

BBC Books, an imprint of Ebury Publishing

20 Vauxhall Bridge Road

London SW1V 2SA

BBC Books is part of the Penguin Random House group of companies whose addresses can be found at global.penguinrandomhouse.com

First published by BBC Books in 2024

www.penguin.co.uk

A CIP catalogue record for this book is available from the British Library

ISBN 9781785948664

With thanks to: Harriet Frost, Nicola Fitzgerald, Caroline Hall, Sarah James, Kate Jones, Clemmie Kirby, Phoebe Lindsley, Ross Morgan, Kate Shane, Stuart Snaith, Showtown Blackpool Museum and Leanne Whitcoop.
Project Editor: Céline Nyssens
Production: Antony Heller
Historical Picture Research: Thomas Carter

Design: Clarkevanmeurs Design

Printed and bound in Germany by Mohn Media Mohndruck GmbH

The authorised representative in the EEA is Penguin Random House Ireland, Morrison Chambers, 32 Nassau Street, Dublin D02 YH68.

MAGIC MOMENTS AND MEMORIES FROM THE WORLD CAPITAL OF DANCE

ALISON MALONEY

CONTENTS

CHAPTER 1
Building the Ballroom 6

CHAPTER 2
Secrets of the Tower 32

CHAPTER 3
Keeping up Appearances 50

CHAPTER 4
Wonderland of Dance 66

CHAPTER 5
Strictly Comes to Town 88

CHAPTER 6
Showtime 126

CHAPTER 7
Getting the Look 152

CHAPTER 8
Backstage in the Ballroom 172

CHAPTER 9
Blackpool Memories 192

CHAPTER 10
When Blackpool Rocks 206

Author's Acknowledgements 224

CHAPTER

1

Building the Ballroom

Once described as 'the most handsome and artistic ballroom in the world', the Blackpool Tower Ballroom transports visitors to an age of glamour and grandeur with its breathtaking interiors from the moment they walk in. From the high arched ceiling to the gold-leafed balconies, plush red seating and famous sprung dance floor, the sheer opulence of the building is the reason why the Tower Ballroom has been a favourite venue for dancers for over 125 years.

Situated at the base of the Tower itself, the original ballroom, the Tower Pavilion, opened in 1894 but proved so popular that, within five years, the owners decided to go bigger and better. They invested in a huge overhaul designed by renowned designer Frank Matcham, and today the Ballroom is considered his most important surviving work.

The interior, which the Theatres Trust says 'conveys an impression of quite staggering opulence', is a sumptuous mix of deep-red upholstery, elegant pillars and gold leaf.

Two tiers of balconies cover three sides of the Ballroom, with the upper layer on the two side walls accommodating bowed boxes, while the stage-facing wall has three balconies. Further onion-domed boxes flank the proscenium arch of the orchestra stage and lighting is provided by two large and 14 smaller Edwardian crystal chandeliers, which hang across the auditorium.

High above the dance floor, which is made from blocks of walnut, mahogany and oak, the segmented arched ceiling boasts exquisite murals framed by ornate gold-leafed plasterwork. In fact, the Ballroom contains so much gold there used to be a team of six specialist gold-leafers on the payroll. When Blackpool Council bought the complex from private owners in 2010, £30,000 of gold leaf was found in the safe. During a recent refurbishment, when gold-leafers were brought in to restore the works, it was weighed and found to be worth £200,000.

Above: *A crowd eagerly lining the streets to witness the laying of the foundation stone of Blackpool Tower, 1891*

Right: *A newspaper caricature featuring John Bickerstaffe, who served as Mayor of Blackpool from 1889–1891*

Opening of an Attraction

The foundation stone of Blackpool Tower was laid by local MP Sir Matthew White Ridley, on 25 September 1891, at an elaborate ceremony.

Also in attendance was Sir John Bickerstaffe, who was both the Mayor of Blackpool and the chairman of the Blackpool Tower Company, which had bought existing attractions on the site, including an aquarium (which stayed open throughout construction), from original owner Dr Cocker.

AQUARIUM
AQUARIUM
AVIARY
LIONS.
AQUARIUM

The Tower Aquarium, pictured here in c. 1890. The aquarium, which was originally called Doctor Cocker's Menagerie, opened in 1874

Legend has it that Bickerstaffe was inspired by a visit to Paris in 1889, where he saw the Eiffel Tower, but this seems to be a myth. However, the construction of the famous Parisian landmark, for the Universal Exhibition of that year, inspired plans for six similar tourist attractions in Britain over the following decade, in Wembley, Brighton, the Isle of Man, Morecambe, New Brighton and Blackpool. Only the latter two were fully constructed after the businessmen behind the scheme ran off with the money that had been invested in the idea. Undaunted, John Bickerstaffe and his associates decided to continue with plans for the Blackpool construction.

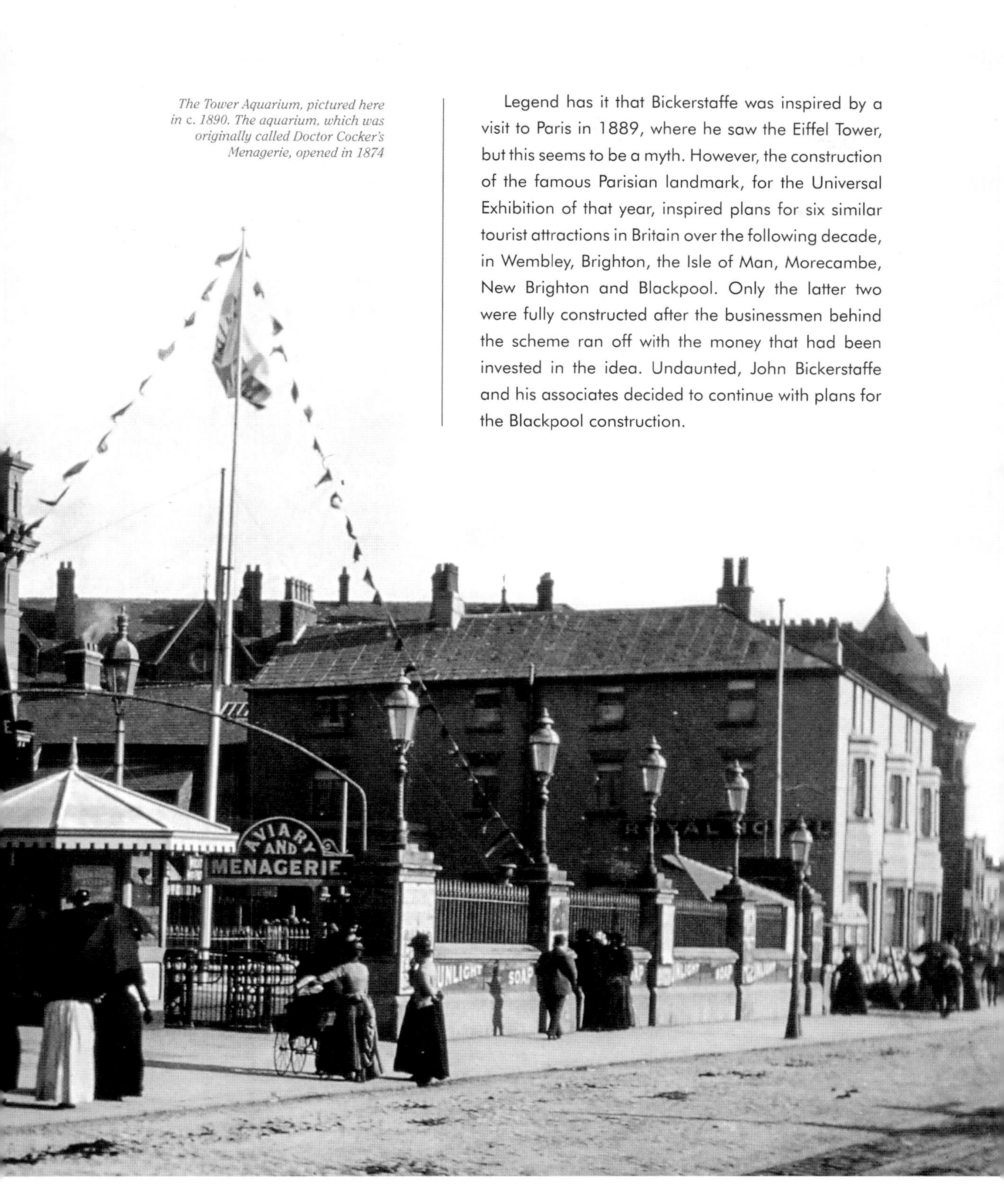

The Blackpool Tower under construction in 1893

Manchester architects James Maxwell and Charles Tuke designed the Tower complex, although neither lived to see their dream come to fruition, and Blackpool builders James Cardwell & Sons laid the brickwork for the buildings while Heenan & Froude constructed the steel tower itself.

Even after the foundation stone was laid, Bickerstaffe and the Blackpool Tower Company struggled to raise the funds for the ambitious complex. In an interview with the *Blackpool Herald*, six months after the opening, Bickerstaffe said: 'There were hundreds of people, even in Blackpool, who said the Tower would never be built, if it was it would never stand, and if it did it would never pay. If anyone had told me three years ago what I would have to go through, I would never have undertaken the position of Chairman, not for a pension, not for £1,000 a year.'

Bickerstaffe ploughed in £20,000 of his own capital, bolstering faith in the project, and negotiated a lower purchase price for the land from the Debenture Corporation, which held the leasehold. He then sold shares to investors, raising £300,000 from 3,000 individuals. Due to investment from textile merchants, John Bickerstaffe quipped that the Tower had been built on bales of cotton – a joke that was taken literally for some years afterwards! In fact, it's built on Nori stone, which also shores up the Empire State Building in New York.

The Tower opening, on 14 May 1894, was met with less fanfare than the laying of the first stone but was hugely popular nonetheless, with around 70,000 people streaming through the door.

The basic ticket, costing sixpence, allowed access to the original attractions as well as the Roof Gardens, Ye Olde English Village, the Ballroom, where afternoon concerts could be enjoyed, and the Monkey House and Menagerie, which housed chimpanzees, mandrills, crocodiles, turtles, bears, cheetahs, hyenas, leopards, lions, a black panther, porcupines, sloths and tigers. A further sixpence would allow visitors to visit the top of the Tower in ground-breaking hydraulic lifts, which proved a huge success, with an estimated 3,000 people taking the ascent during opening day.

The *British Architect* magazine noted that about 500 people an hour were taken to the top, where there was 'promenading space' for over 100, and that the 'elevator worked in the smoothest possible fashion the day through'. It added: 'A splendid view may be obtained from the top of the Tower and at favourable times the Isle of Man, Southport, Liverpool, Barrow, Preston, Blackburn, Chorley and surrounding towns can plainly be distinguished.'

As well as tea rooms and refreshment areas, musical entertainment was offered by a string quartet in the Roof Gardens and a military band in Ye Olde English Village. The 30-strong Tower Orchestra played in the spacious ballroom, named the Grand Pavilion, which had capacity for 6,000 guests.

With the Tower entertainment venue proving a roaring success, the rival Winter Gardens fought back with the opening of the grand Empress Ballroom and Indian Lounge, in 1896. One of the largest ballrooms in the world, with a floor area of 12,500 square feet (1,161 square metres), the Empress was designed by Mangnall & Littlewood, and featured an impressive semi-circular ceiling, divided into panels decorated with ceramic designs of mermaids, seaweed and fish. A gigantic Ferris wheel, measuring 220 feet (67 metres), completed the revamped entertainment complex.

Above: *The original Blackpool Tower Ballroom, pictured before the renovation that happened in 1899*

Patrons enjoying a glamorous evening at the Empress Ballroom, photographed by the Saidman brothers in 1936

ROTARY
INTERNATIONAL

Above: *The Empress Ballroom photographed by the Saidman Brothers in 1936*

Above: *The entrance to the Winter Gardens, 1880*

Tower Inferno

A year later, on 22 July, the Tower suffered a major setback when a fire broke out on one of the landings. Excited locals gathered round as flames licked the top of the attraction. According to a report in the *Liverpool Mercury* published two days later: 'Showers of sparks flew around in all directions, and large pieces of blazing wood dropped away from the burning mass, and sped through the air like rockets. As the flames got better hold of the woodwork, the heat became more and more intense, and long before midnight the iron framework on the east side of the platform was white heat.'

Above: *The Empress Ballroom, photographed by the Saidman Brothers during the 1936 Blackpool Dance Festival*

The article noted that the only person hurt in the blaze was John Warmsley, the keeper of the Menagerie and Aquarium, 'whose hands were badly burnt, and who narrowly escaped losing his life' as he bravely rescued animals, birds and fish from the building. The worst damage was caused by a huge iron counterweight from the hydraulic lifts, weighing 11 tons, which crashed through a glass roof below and into the Circus ring located in the base of the Tower, damaging some of the ironwork

Left: *A rare photograph of the Blackpool Tower ablaze in 1897*

on the way. The report continued: 'About half-past eleven a terrific crash was heard, practically awakening the whole town, and the residents and visitors poured out of their houses in hundreds and thousands until the streets in the neighbourhood became almost as thronged as though it were midday.' The counterweight, in the north-west leg of the Tower, smashed into one of the two royal boxes in the Circus. Too heavy to remove, the huge weight remains in the corner of the Circus to this day, boxed in and hidden with mirrors. Remarkably, the Tower building opened as usual the following day, with only the ascent to the viewing platform out of commission.

'The trains arrived yesterday with extraordinary loads of passengers, but there was great disappointment at finding the Tower apparently unchanged,' reported the *Liverpool Mercury*. 'The structure of the Tower itself is practically uninjured, not even the paint having been scorched below the point where the fire originated on the 380 feet [116 metre] landing.'

Matcham Renovation

Facing increased competition from the Winter Gardens, John Bickerstaffe called in renowned architect and designer Frank Matcham, already responsible for numerous theatres across the UK, including three in London, as well as the Grand Theatre, Blackpool, and the Norwich Theatre Royal.

Modelled on the Rococo style of the Louis XV period, the lavish revamp used a colour scheme described in the Tower guide of 1899 as 'delicate shades of cream, green, blue, grey, and old gold of the Renaissance period, relieved with pure English gold'. The ambitious design was conceived on an unprecedented scale, with a floor measuring over 12,000 square feet (1,115 square metres), surrounded by seating areas for spectators. The roof was raised by 15 feet (5 metres) and the balconies were also placed higher, allowing seating for 800 to be added to a gallery below, while the auditorium was also extended. The arched ceiling rose from a false-galleried cornice, supported by winged female figures, and was split into gold-framed sections, depicting scenes from a masked ball.

Below: *An intricate mural depicting a masked ball on the ceiling of the Ballroom*

Opposite: *The beautiful gold cornices decorating the Ballroom roof*

Supporting the roof were green marble columns spaced around the outside of the room and on either side of the stage. One of the most innovative features was a sliding roof, measuring 50 feet by 20 feet (15 metres by 15 metres), for use in warm weather. The only one in Blackpool, according to the Tower's 1899 guide, 'the roof slides in two halves and is arranged so as to be opened or closed in half a minute'. In 2010, when Blackpool Council took control of the building, plans to restore the mechanism were unveiled. Carl Carrington, of Blackpool Council, said: 'It's an interesting piece of Victorian engineering, an ingenious way of air conditioning the ballroom. The idea was that you could slide the roof back, and not only were you dancing under the stars, but all of this hot air from the ballroom was escaping through the hole, and cold air pouring in from the sides directly on to the dancers below. 'The Ballroom's luxurious splendour was crowned with an elaborate proscenium arch, at the east end of the building, which towers 35 feet (11 metres) above the dance floor, and bears the inscription 'Bid me discourse, I will enchant thine ear'.

Closed for almost a year, the new and improved Ballroom reopened on 30 March 1899, with the illustrated guide boasting: 'The ballroom is at once a palace and a work of art, and the Tower Company has every justification, therefore, for declaring it to be the most magnificently decorated ballroom in Europe.'

Today, the stunning Ballroom continues to attract visitors from all over the world. Kate Shane, Regional Director of the Merlin Entertainments group, the current operators of the Tower Ballroom, says: 'I may be biased but in terms of a venue of this scale, where you can just come in and sit or dance, there's nothing else like it, it's incredible.'

Above: *The inscription above the stage of the Tower Ballroom, which comes from the Shakespeare poem 'Venus and Adonis'*

RSE, I WILL ENCHANT THINE EAR

Left and above:
Local girls dancing and chatting with RAF soldiers stationed in Blackpool, 1943

Wartime Service

While tea dances and ballroom competitions have always been at the heart of the building's purpose, the vast space came in useful during the Second World War. During the day, the Ballroom was used for military drills, with the space, along with other Blackpool venues, used to train 600,000 airmen from the UK, the US and other allied countries preparing for D-Day. It was also used for sewing parachutes, with swathes of silk spread out across the polished wood floor.

In the evening, the dancing resumed, with many of the soldiers billeted in the local area rushing to meet the local girls.

Fire and Restoration

Catastrophe struck once again, this time in the Tower Ballroom itself, in December 1956 when a cigarette discarded from the top balcony sparked a devastating fire. Blackpool firefighters, joined by crews from two neighbouring areas, battled the blaze for five hours and, with the help of southerly winds, prevented the spread to the rest of the building, but the iconic dance floor and the restaurant below were destroyed. A report in the local paper, the *Gazette*, lamented the damage to the complex, which had been dubbed 'The Wonderland of the World' in 1935. 'Inside was a scene of desolation and destruction,' read the report. 'The north end of the famous "Wonderland of the World" was a grim waste of smoke, running water, charred wood and fire hoses.' A Tower executive at the time estimated the damage at around £250,000 – around £7 million today.

Above and right: *Damage inflicted on the Tower Ballroom and its ceiling by the second fire at the Blackpool Tower, 1956*

BALFE
GRIEG
AUBER

'The Tower Ballroom is iconic and beautifully ornate. Frank Matcham was a very famous Victorian theatre designer so the Ballroom is based on the elaborate theatres favoured at the time, with the proscenium arch, the boxes and all the gilding, but rather than having the stalls in there, they worked in a dance floor. It's an iconic dance floor as well, with a unique design and beautifully sprung. It's an incredible building.'

Anton Du Beke

While many saw the disastrous fire as a chance to redesign and modernise, Douglas Bickerstaffe, who had followed in his father John's footsteps as the Managing Director of the Tower Company, insisted Matcham's iconic Ballroom be restored to its former glory. Renowned French art director Andrew Mazzei was persuaded out of retirement to carefully restore the building back to its former splendour, reinstating the ornamental gold-leaf features and the fire-damaged murals.

The ceiling, carefully reconstructed with murals repainted by local artist Peter Miller, took over a year to complete. Entirely destroyed in the fire, the dance floor got more of an upgrade, taking three months to build with over 30,000 blocks of mahogany, oak and walnut laid and polished. The iconic sprung floor also gained a mechanism, which allowed the springs to be locked for theatre shows and non-dance events, to minimise the bounce. In all, the restoration took two years and cost double the original estimate, at £500,000. The skilled craftsmen used 170 tonnes (170,000 kilograms) of plaster, 100 gallons (455 litres) of paint remover, 600 gallons (2,728 litres) of paint, 1,000 yards (914 metres) of metallic gold wallpaper imported from Switzerland, and 9,500 square feet (883 square metres) of gold leaf.

On the reopening, on 28 May 1958, the *Gazette* reported: 'Matcham's original vision and decoration was restored, magnificent as it ever was since its opening.' Beneath the Ballroom, however, the dining area took a different direction, with full modernisation. Now called the Tower Lounge, the modern café-style restaurant was designed by James Bell with seating for over 1,000.

Fun Facts

- The construction of the steel Tower led engineers Heenan & Froude to design the first electric crane in the world, in 1893.
- The Tower took 5 million bricks, 2,500 tonnes (2,500,000 kilograms) of iron and 93 tonnes (93,000 kilograms) of cast steel to build.
- Blackpool Tower is the only building in the world that has three Frank Matcham-designed areas: the Circus, the Tower Ballroom and a third that was part of the Tower's Oriental Village and China Tea Houses. The ballroom floor measures 120 feet by 102 feet (37 metres by 31 metres) – which is nine times bigger than the *Strictly Come Dancing* studio floor in Elstree. However, for the *Strictly Come Dancing* Blackpool pecial some of this floor is used for seating the audience.
- The unique sprung dance floor is made up of 30,602 separate blocks of mahogany, oak and walnut.
- The bounce in the floor is created by 21 sets of leaf springs, similar to those used in car suspension. They can be tightened and loosened through a hatch in the floor, to adjust the springiness.
- The names of 16 composers are to be found around the Ballroom, etched into the plaster and embellished with gold leaf.
- The inscription above the Ballroom stage reads, 'Bid me discourse, I will enchant thine ear', and is taken from the Shakespeare poem 'Venus and Adonis'.

CHAPTER

2

This page: *The Blackpool Tower, dubbed 'The Wonderland of the World', photographed in 1936*

Secrets of the Tower

The magnificent Tower Ballroom has always been part of a huge entertainment complex, where families have flocked to have fun since it first drew the crowds in 1894. A sign installed in 1935 on the Tower promenade declared the venue 'The Wonderland of the World', and the imposing building hides a multitude of marvels.

The Mighty Wurlitzer

The Tower Ballroom has two organs in place, and both are played on a daily basis. The first, a Roland, is permanently on stage, but its more famous big brother, the Mighty Wurlitzer, rises out of the stage every hour, on the hour, while an organist plays. The magnificent instrument was built in 1939, to the specification of the legendary Reginald Dixon, resident organist from March 1930 to March 1970.

Above: *Reginald Dixon sitting at the Mighty Wurlitzer, 1951*

Reginald was hired to play the organ at the Tower Ballroom after two in-house organists, Max Bruce and James Hodgetts, struggled to keep up the correct tempo for dancing on a previous instrument, a 2/10 Wurlitzer. Reginald was given a trial, with the proviso that if he couldn't make the organ work for dancing, both he and the 2/10 Wurlitzer would go. Reginald was such a success that he soon outgrew the instrument, and the Tower commissioned the Mighty Wurlitzer theatre organ, which was bigger and specifically designed by their talented organist. The smaller 2/10 Wurlitzer was moved to the Empress Ballroom in Blackpool's Winter Gardens, where it is still playing today.

Reginald's distinctive bouncy recitals became famous throughout the land, through BBC radio broadcasts from the Tower Ballroom, encapsulating 'the Blackpool sound'. Over a 50-year career Reginald sold more recordings of his music than any other organist, before or since, and his sales ranked alongside the likes of contemporaries Bing Crosby and Victor Silvester. During his 40-year tenure, Reginald's only extended break away from the Ballroom was during the Second World War, when he enlisted and was temporarily replaced with Ena Baga, the only female organist in the venue's history.

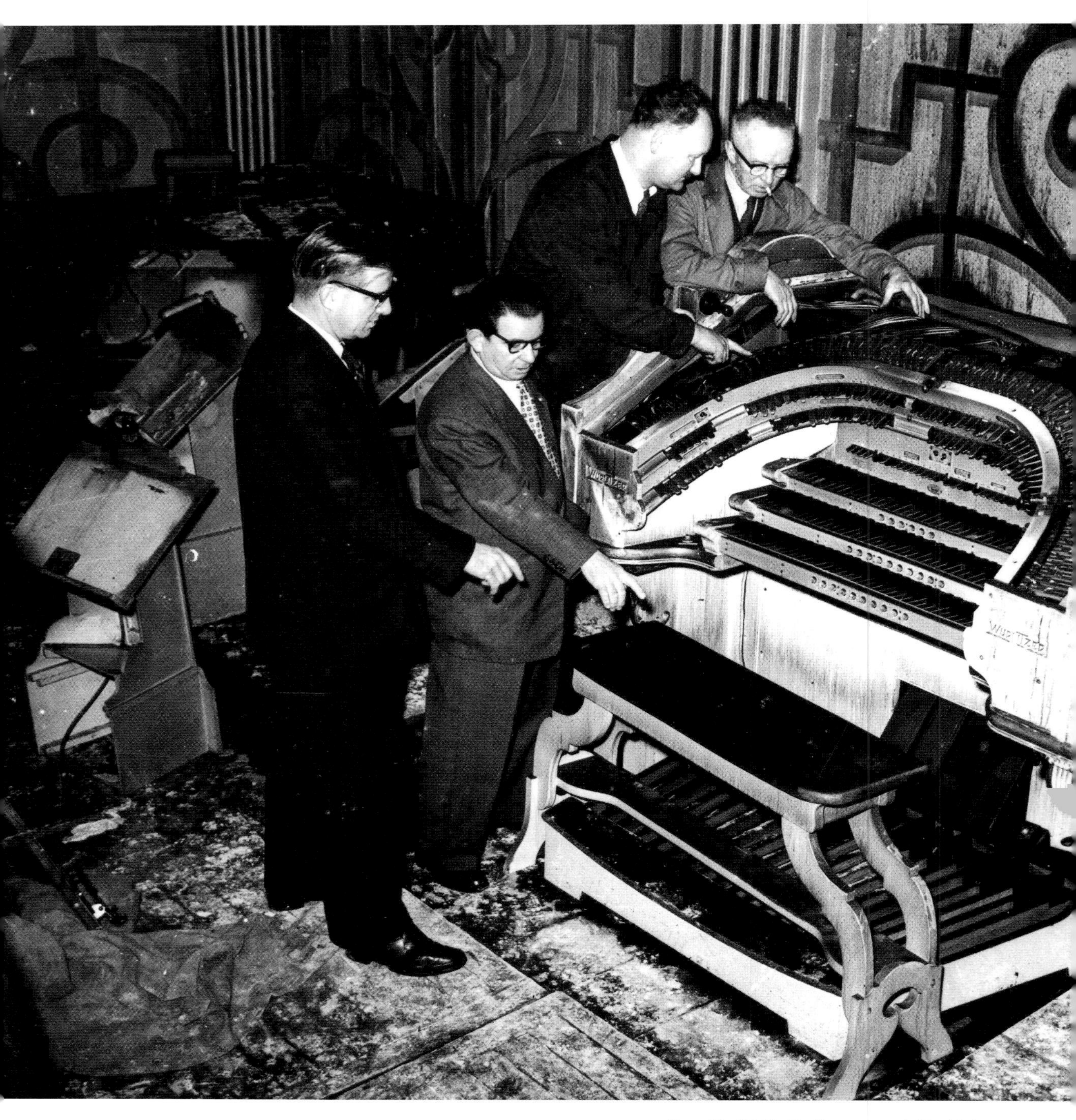

Above: *The Mighty Wurlitzer surrounded by debris from the fire at the Blackpool Tower, 1956*

Incredibly, the Mighty Wurlitzer lived up to its name during the 1956 fire, surviving unscathed.

Today, the team of resident organists is led by Phil Kelsall, who has played at the venue since 1975, initially with the Tower Circus Band, taking over as organist in the Ballroom in 1977. In 2010, he was awarded an MBE for what was described as a '35-year love affair' with the Blackpool Tower Ballroom. 'I have played nearly every theatre organ in Britain, but with the fine acoustics of the Blackpool Tower Ballroom, the [Mighty] Wurlitzer makes a totally unique sound and in my opinion is one of the finest ever built by Wurlitzer,' he says, adding that he still loves the moment when he rises out of the stage to delight the dancers on the floor. 'I do sometimes think, as I'm halfway through the stage, what a strange way of earning a living!'

Above: *Phil Kelsall sitting at the Mighty Wurlitzer, 2018*

Below: *A poster advertising circus acts at the Blackpool Tower, 1899*

Right: *The famous water finale, photographed in 1956*

The Circus

Beneath the famous dance floor, nestled between the four giant legs of the Tower, lies a hidden treasure in the Tower Circus, where the Endresz family have been putting on daily shows for 30 years. Opened as part of the main complex in 1894, with a separate admission price of 6d. (sixpence) – equivalent to £3 today – it is the oldest permanent circus arena in the world and has never missed a season.

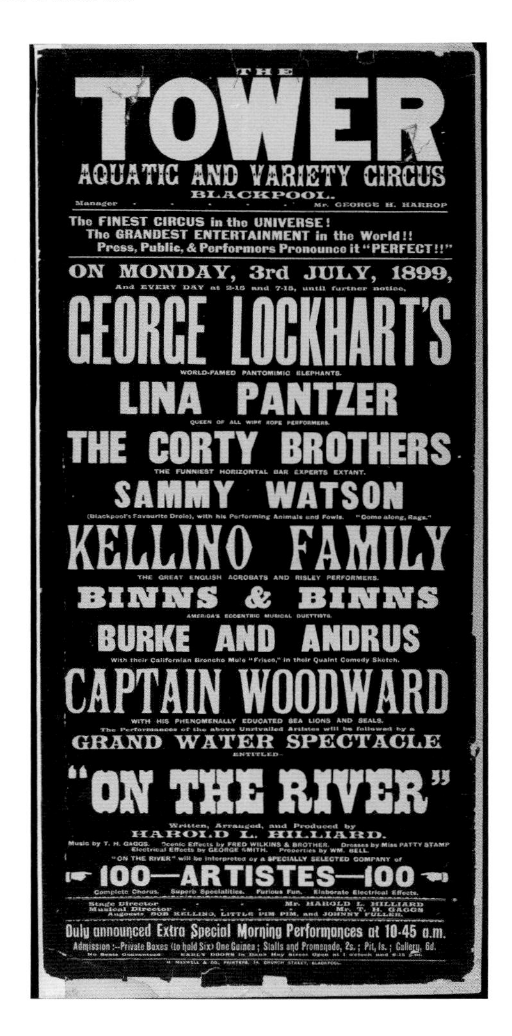

Also designed by Frank Matcham, it is as ornate as the Ballroom, although very different in style, with an Oriental and Moorish influence, reputed to stem from the architect's travels to the Alhambra palace in Spain. The magnificent marble entrance led into a 'crush room' with wood-panelled walls and then into the main auditorium, a riot of red and gold, with a domed ceiling and gold leaf decorating the iron legs of the tower itself.

After the Matcham revamp, the *Blackpool Gazette* commented: 'The pit, the gallery and every part of the circus is ornamented with infinite variety indeed, but in a manner completely harmonious with the style adopted ... The general appearance embodies all that light, graceful beauty peculiar to the architecture of the East.'

The arena, measuring 110 feet by 110 feet (34 metres by 34 metres), has seating for an audience of 1,300 people and the central stage features a hydraulic floor that sinks and fills with 42,000 gallons (190,936 litres) of water in less than a minute – to a depth of 4 feet 6 inches (1.4 metres) – for the spectacular water finale, which has concluded every performance since the very first show.

The Circus featured wild animals until as recently as 1991, with performing polar bears, four elephants, and numerous lions and tigers, which lived in the building. The spectacle of elephants being marched over the road to the beach, to wash in the Irish Sea, became a familiar sight to locals – although this was thought to be more of a PR stunt than a ritual to benefit the animals. Over the winter months, between 1930 and 1960, many of the animals, including the polar bears, were moved to an area of land in nearby Staining, which housed pens where they could be let outside as well as a circus ring for rehearsals.

One of the maintenance staff who has worked at the Tower for over 30 years remembers an occasion when they didn't secure the lions' cage at night in the 1980s. 'The Tower is manned 24 hours a day and the staff carry out hourly checks in each area through the night,' says Kate. 'One night [the member of staff] completed his hourly checks, went back to the control room and was having a cup of tea and reading his newspaper when he heard a noise. He looked up and there was a lion the other side of the glass. The trainers had to come down and get them back into the cage and when they arrived, the lions were just prowling around the Circus seats.'

A sea lion pool was installed on the roof, and during the watery finale, they would shoot down slides and into the flooded ring.

In 1990 Sir Bernard Delfont, CEO of the Blackpool Tower at the time, banned animals from the show at the request of his wife, a keen animal rights campaigner.

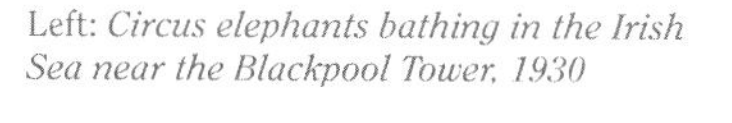

Left: *Circus elephants bathing in the Irish Sea near the Blackpool Tower, 1930*

Circus Acts

Resident ringmasters included George Lockhart, from 1914 to 1945, who first performed in the ring at the age of six. Norman Barrett, famed for his bareback riding and his performing budgies, took the role for 25 years from 1966 and, in 1990, was the subject of *This Is Your Life*, after being surprised by Michael Aspel and his Big Red Book. He went on to run Zippos Circus and was awarded an MBE in 2010.

Below left: *George Lockhart photographed c.1931*
Below right: *Norman Barrett after receiving his MBE, 2010*

Top: *One of the performers from Australian aerialists The 6 Flying De Pauls, 1958*

Above left: *American trick cyclists act The Theron Troupe, 1960*

Above right: *Human statue act The Golden Linders, performing during the Water Fantasy finale, 1957*

Among many others, acts who performed at the circus included the Australian aerialist group The Six Flying De Pauls, the American trick cyclists The Theron Troupe, the German roller skating act The Dubowys and Italian trick cyclists the Biasinis. The Flying Wallendas, a world-renowned acrobatic high-wire act who performed without safety nets, also appeared there in 1939.

Above: *German Roller skating act The Dubowys, 1959*
Right: *Italian trick cyclists The Biasinis, 1965*

A resident clown has always been attached to the Blackpool Tower Circus. Among the first was Bob Kellino, who performed from 1897 to 1903, and, between the wars, Doodles and his sidekick Austin was a hugely popular act.

THE TOWER CIRCUS.

Manager: Mr. G. H. Harrop.

30th JUNE, 1902. PROGRAMME. At 2-30 and 7-30.

No.	Artiste's Name.	Time.
1	The Famous Turkish Horse— "ABDALLAH" Trained and Introduced by Mr. Franz Cariot.	2-30 and 7-30
2	Barrel Jumping Extraordinary, by the BROTHERS AUGUSTIN	2-40 and 7-40
3	An Amusing Entree by BOB KELLINO & PIM-PIM Blackpool's Bundles of Fun.	2-50 and 7-50
4	Novel Club Juggling Speciality, by FITZGERALD AND THE SISTERS ROMA Entitled—AMERICAN SWELLS AT PRACTICE.	3-5 and 8-5
5	The Unique Musical Eccentrics— MARTINETTI & GROSSI Introducing Their Latest Novelty—"The Musical Bicycle."	3-22 and 8-22
6	The One-Legged Wonders of the World, THE DONATOS The Only Jumpers of their class on Earth.	3-39 and 8-39
7	For the First Time in England, Herr Ed. Wulff's Original PONY ORCHESTRA The only one in existence. Trained and Introduced by Mr. Franz Cariot.	3-52 and 8-52
8	Madame Lizett's Original LADY CYCLE SENSATION	4-12 and 9-12
9	A Trio of Muscular Marvels, THE SAXONS including ARTHUR SAXON, who claims to be the Strongest Man in the World.	4-30 and 9-30
10	PROF. JAMES FINNEY (Champion All Round Swimmer of the World), MISS MARIE FINNEY (The Heroine of London Bridge), and the Misses MAUD, ELSIE and GLADYS FINNEY	[illegible] and 9-45

Augusts - - BOB KELLINO and LITTLE PIM-PIM.

Stage Director - - Mr. HAROLD L. HILLIARD

Musical Director - - Mr. H. S. PARKER

THIS PROGRAMME IS SUBJECT TO SLIGHT ALTERATION

The most famous, however was Charlie Cairoli, an Italian clown who made his debut in 1939, along with his father Jeanne-Marie. Interned on the Isle of Man for the duration of the Second World War, he returned to the Tower Circus in 1945 and stayed until his retirement in 1979. In 1970, he was the subject of *This Is Your Life*, who called him the 'king of clowns', and he also had a long-running children's show, *Right Charlie!*

Below: *Charlie Cairoli whipping up a delighted audience into laughter, 1954*

Above right: *A programme for the Blackpool Tower Circus mentioning Bob Kellino, 1902*

Mooky has been the resident clown since 1991. The son of director Laci Endresz, who shares his name, he first started performing as a clown at the age of four and was juggling flaming torches by the time he was 12. His sidekick is brother Tom – aka Bubu – who performs under the name Mr Boo.

The Endresz family took over the Circus in 1991 and have been entertaining generations of fans for over three decades. Director and producer Laci Endresz Sr was born in Hungary in 1945, the sixth generation of a circus family. He graduated from the Hungarian Circus Academy and spent 25 years perfecting the flying trapeze. Laci's wife, Maureen, also comes from a long line of circus performers. Her father, Bobby Roberts, began his career at the Tower Circus, with brother Tommy and their wives, in a bareback riding troupe called the Ottawas. They went on to establish their own circus. The couple met when Laci was performing for Maureen's family's circus, in 1970. Their three children followed their parents into the ring.

With generations of performers on both sides, the family are highly regarded in the circus world, and in 2009, they were asked to train Take That for a dance routine in which they dressed as clowns for their world tour.

Above: *Mooky, the resident clown at Blackpool Tower Circus, photographed next to his brother, Mr Boo*

Above: *An illustration of the aquarium by MD Morgan that featured in Blackpool Tower programmes* c. *1926*

Right: *The menagerie, photographed in 1900*

The Aquarium

Dr Cocker's Aquarium, Aviary and Menagerie predated the Tower by 20 years, opening in 1874. It was kept open during construction to keep a steady revenue stream coming in, and became incorporated into the new building. Modelled on Derbyshire caverns, the ground-floor attraction greeted the visitor with tanks full of marine creatures from around the world.

By the time it closed in 2010, the huge aquarium housed almost 60 species of fresh-water and salt-water fish in numerous tanks, the largest of which held 7,040 gallons (32,000 litres) of water.

Monkey House and Menagerie

The Tower's famed zoo boasted a number of exotic animals at the opening of the complex, and by 1904, the collection was considered one of the most extensive in the country. The reptile enclosure housed crocodiles and turtles as well as porcupines, sloths, bears, cheetahs, hyenas, leopards, lions, tigers and a black panther. A huge variety of primates filled the Monkey House and the daily chimpanzees' tea party was a huge draw for visitors.

The animals' keeper was Jim Walmsley, who lived in the Tower, in rooms adjacent to the Menagerie, with his wife Hannah and their children, so he was available day and night. A devoted keeper, he was described as having 'a wide knowledge of wild beasts and various kinds of fish'. In the 1901 Census he listed his occupation as 'Superintendent of Wild Beasts'. Jim was also responsible for breeding programmes and, according to the *Blackpool Gazette*, he was 'never so happy as when he had a litter of lion cubs in his kitchen'.

The Tower zoo closed to the public in 1969 and, at the behest of Blackpool Council, plans were drawn up for a local attraction to house the animals. Four years later, they were moved to the new Blackpool Zoo on East Park Drive.

The Roof Gardens

Situated on level six of the Tower, the Roof Gardens were modelled on The Crystal Palace, with a wide glass ceiling supported by ornamental ironwork, a rock garden, towering palm trees and exotic plants. Used as an entertainment space, as well as an area to relax, the gardens played host to variety performances and concerts.

The Aviary, which housed many rare birds, was also on level six along with the smaller reptiles. In 1977, the smaller animals' menagerie and Roof Gardens were closed, becoming Jungle Jim's Adventure Playground – named in tribute to Jim Walmsley.

Above: *The Tower Roof Gardens photographed* c.*1910*

Fun Facts

- The Tower's height is 518 feet and 9 inches (158.12 metres). On a clear day it can be seen from as far away as Wales and the Lake District.
- There are 563 steps from the roof of the Tower building to the top, which the maintenance teams use for the structure's upkeep.
- On opening, the complex included shop units initially occupied by two milliners, two confectioners, a cutler, a tobacconist, a bootmaker, a ship dealer and a hairdresser.
- W. C. Fields worked as a juggler for one season in the Circus, before he became a Hollywood star.
- In 1914, an underground passage was opened between the Tower and the Palace Theatre, so that acts could perform at both on the same night.
- In the Second World War, a radar station was located at the top of the Tower and RAF servicemen surveyed the Irish Sea from their unique vantage point.
- There are 5 miles (8 kilometres) of cables supplying electricity to the 10,000 light bulbs that illuminate the Tower.
- Painting the Tower takes seven years and the workers who carry out the external maintenance are affectionately known as 'Stick men'.
- The top of the Tower was painted silver in 1977 as part of Queen Elizabeth II's Silver Jubilee celebrations.
- If winds exceed 45 miles per hour, the top of the Tower is closed for safety reasons. In gusts above 70 miles per hour, the top sways an inch.
- In 1992, the complex was briefly renamed Tower World and was opened by Diana, Princess of Wales.
- In October 2019, the Countess of Wessex visited the building and was treated to afternoon tea in the centre of the Circus ring.
- In 1998, the infamous 'walk of faith', a glass floor at the top of the Tower, opened. Originally made from two sheets of laminated glass, 2 inches (2.5 centimetres) thick, it was reinforced during the 2011 refurbishment and can now hold the weight of two elephants!

CHAPTER

3

Welcome to

The Blackpool Towe

Ballroom

Welcome to
The Blackpool Tower
Ballroom

Keeping up Appearances

As well as the *Strictly Come Dancing* Blackpool special, the Tower Ballroom hosts an average of 80 events a year. In between events, the venue is open to the public every day except Christmas Day and a fortnight in January.

'The two-week closure is for maintenance of the chandeliers, the dance floor and the Wurlitzer organ,' says Kate Shane, General Manager of the Blackpool Tower. 'The chandeliers are hand-winched down, restored and repaired, the bulbs are checked, then they are cleaned and serviced and hand-winched back up to the ceiling.' Organ specialist Keith Ledson has been servicing the Wurlitzer organ since 1979, and he uses this time to check the 1,034 pipes and make any repairs and adjustments needed. The maintenance team then restore anything else that is affected by the wear and tear of human contact, such as the upholstery. The lower levels are also redecorated and the dance floor is re-polished.

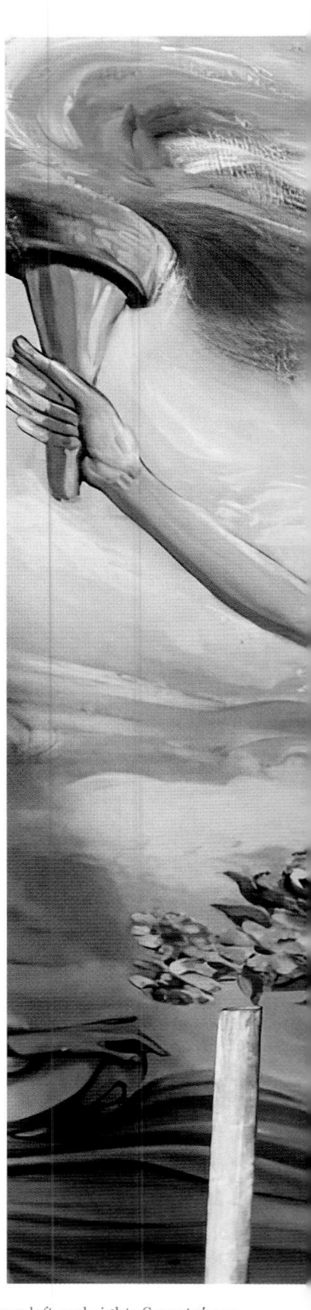

In 2020, the pandemic closed the Tower Ballroom for the first time in its history, providing an opportunity for a more extensive programme of restoration. The project received £764,000 from the Government's Culture Recovery Fund, together with funding from Blackpool Council, which took the total amount to £1.1 million. The work began in 2021, and over a period of six months, a team of 30 artisans worked tirelessly to restore the intricate plasterwork, gold leaf and murals as well as the iconic dance floor, replicating the skills of the original craftspeople of 1894. Before carrying out the detailed work, 12 square spaces were drilled into the ceiling to establish the exact methodology used in the original construction by exposing the materials, so it could be mirrored by the twenty-first-century workers. Among the methods was the rare art of fibrous plastering, using organic hessian imported from India mixed with 2 tonnes (2,000 kilograms) of plaster, to repair intricate plasterwork on the proscenium arch and the ballroom ceiling.

'It took two weeks to construct the scaffolding from the dance floor right to the ceiling, then these amazing skilled people turned up and started doing additional fixings, and restoring the painting and the gold leaf,' says Kate. 'It was just incredible.'

Above left and right: *Smartphone photographs of the renovations carried out on the Tower Ballroom, 2021*

Above and right:
Workmen carrying out restoration work to the ceiling of the Tower Ballroom, 2021

'The ornate ceiling doesn't get affected by humans, just age. The methods used when it was built means it is very robust, but this was our chance to preserve it and make sure it was going to stand another 130 years.'

The murals, damaged over the years, were restored by artists who colour-matched oil paints using the naked eye, and several hundred litres of gold paint were used to restore the gold-leaf artwork to its former glory. Years of dust collected behind the plaster figures that adorn the ceiling was removed, with dozens of bags-full being taken away each day.

Signatures found under the ceiling murals during the restoration dated the last time workers had access to the space as 1957. Kate and her colleagues also had a rare chance to get up close to the proscenium arch and ceiling they had admired from down below for years.

'We climbed the scaffolding and we got to the top of the proscenium arch – we could touch the three ladies that are part of the arch,' she says. 'It was quite a moment and a colleague said, "If we can ever do this again in our lifetime, something's gone horribly wrong. Let's celebrate this moment as a once-in-a-lifetime." And it was. It's now been secured for future generations to enjoy.'

The dance floor also got a facelift, as Kate explains. 'During the routine maintenance we take a layer of polish off and reapply fresh polish. But this time, we took all of the polish off as well as a fine layer of the wood, so it was completely smooth and flat, and then applied polish. It brought all of the colours out and it just looks spectacular.'

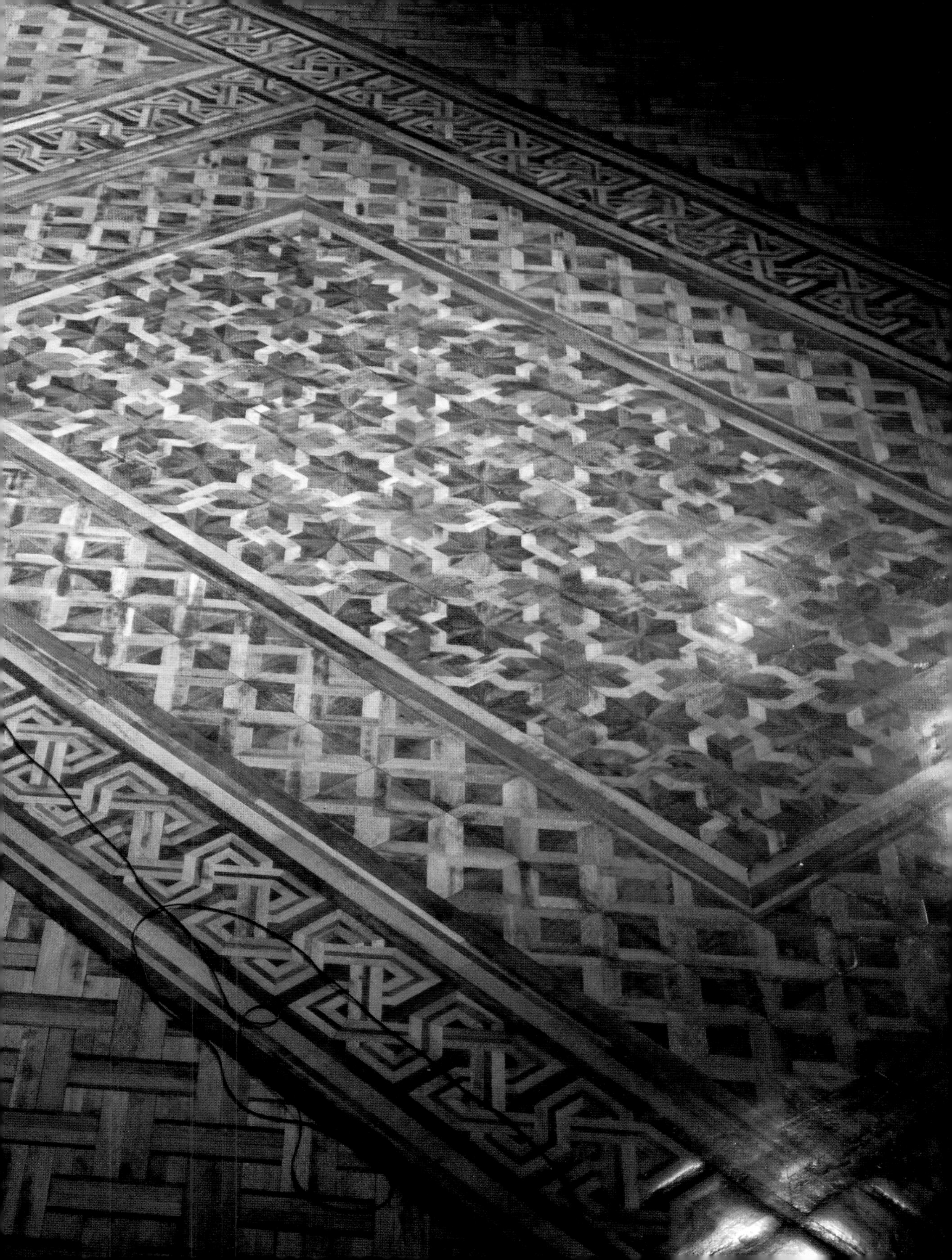

Project Manager Keith Langton, who previously oversaw restoration work in the Queen's Gallery at Buckingham Palace, told news website *LancsLive*: 'I thought Buckingham Palace had the wow factor – which obviously it absolutely did. But working here at the Blackpool Tower Ballroom has blown me away. This really is something else. It is a project I will never forget – and perhaps even a project for me to retire on.

'Everyone wants to end their career on a high – and I don't think I could get a better high than working at the Ballroom. It has been an absolute pleasure and honour!'

In June 2021, the Tower Ballroom reopened to the public for tea dances, entertainment and events, with thousands attending tea dances every year, including regular events for those living with dementia.

'The impact the Ballroom has in the community and also on tourism in the UK is significant,' says Kate. 'As a space that is as beautiful as it is, and as popular as it is, it is also accessible for everybody.

'When people know that you work here, in whatever capacity, they want to share their stories, especially the older generation. They tell me, "I met my husband here in the 1950s," and they come alive as they talk. For those living with dementia, particularly, the memories that are brightest are the ones from when they were younger, so they come back in and they're at the age they were when they had that memory. They just light up.

'When I walk through that space and see the arch with that lovely quote, "Bid me discourse, I will enchant thine ear", and the Wurlitzer is playing for the tea dance and there are little tots dancing on dads' toes, it's just magical. I feel really lucky.'

Below: *Couples enjoying a tea dance in the Tower Ballroom*

Uncovering the Past

The 2021 refurbishment of the ballroom ceiling was carried out by ornamental plaster specialists, whose team found a remarkable haul of historical objects – including century-old newspapers, cigarette packets and an old walking stick – behind the angel figures decorating the ballroom ceiling. The oldest newspaper uncovered was an issue of the *News of the World* dating back to 1911, printed in the same month as the coronation of King George V and his wife Mary, and hailing a forthcoming visit to the seaside town by the new king. Other papers included a *Manchester Evening Chronicle* from 1913, the year Suffragette Emily Wilding Davison was killed at the Epsom Derby, and a *Daily Mail* from 1922.

Some cigarette packets in the ceiling void, which it is believed were left by builders and craftspeople, had been there for a century, with the earliest dating from the nineteenth century and more from both world wars. A number of bottles dating back to the Edwardian era were also found, including a vintage whisky bottle, and a tin of baked beans, likely to have been lunch for one of the workers, was also recovered.

'We can only assume that craftspeople were sat on these steels over 100 years ago, reading the paper and having a cigarette,' says Keith. 'Their waste was tossed into a void and has been preserved almost in a time capsule for our teams to find today.' The artefacts are now on display at Blackpool Tower.

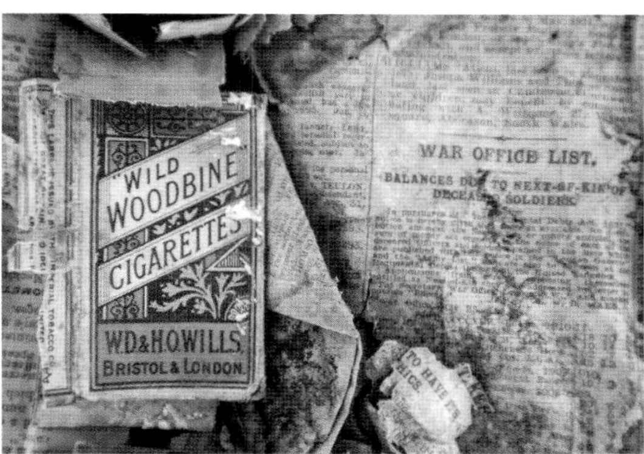

Above: *Artefacts including cigarette packets, advertising materials and newspapers unearthed during the renovations*

Above: *A holiday photo of Kate Shane and her parents at Blackpool Pleasure Beach*

Blackpool Memories

KATE SHANE, General Manager of the Blackpool Tower

'I walked into the Ballroom for the first time as a child because my parents used to bring me to Blackpool on holiday. There was some form of dance competition going on. I remember as a young child being blown away by the scale. The first time I walked into the Ballroom after I joined as General Manager of the Tower, I had worked quite late and I radioed Security Control and asked if there was anybody in the building. Security said I was the only one there, so I went into the Ballroom, dropped my bags, then I walked into the middle of the dance floor, put out my arms and did a twirl. I did several spins around the floor. At the end of it, my head said, "How do you know there's no CCTV?" I went downstairs trying to look all professional, and luckily there wasn't CCTV in there! There is now.

'I've got a lot of emotional attachment to this building. I love the history and the stories that have come out of it. The Tower Ballroom is beautiful, it's accessible, and it's unique. I don't think there's anywhere else like it.'

Fun Facts

- A team of over 30 specialists worked together on the 2021 refurbishment, working a combined 21,000 hours over six months.
- Each worker climbed an average of 85 flights of scaffolding daily.
- Each Edwardian crystal chandelier weighs half a tonne (500 kilograms) and it takes four people to lower each one down for the annual spring clean. They are dusted and wiped, and 1,120 bulbs are individually cleaned and inspected.
- The Tower Ballroom serves over 20,000 afternoon teas a year.

CHAPTER

4

Wonderland of Dance

For over 130 years, Blackpool has been the dance capital of the world, with the most prestigious ballroom and Latin championships taking place in either the Tower Ballroom or the Winter Gardens. As the legendary former Head Judge of *Strictly Come Dancing,* the late Len Goodman, once said, 'There's been dancing in Blackpool for almost as long as there's been sand on the beach. Right from the start Blackpool's known how to party. It's no wonder this place became the spiritual home of ballroom.'

The Tower Ballroom

An early advertising slogan hailed the Tower Ballroom as a place 'Where a factory girl can be a Duchess for the day', and for the hundreds of thousands who have danced on the hallowed dance floor, the sentiment certainly rings true. Early visitors flocked to dance to the music of Oliver Gaggs' orchestra, which played nightly in the Tower Ballroom. Because of the unique sliding roof, fine weather meant couples could dance under the stars when the panel was opened for ventilation.

Left: *Former judges Len Goodman and Darcey Bussell at the Tower Ballroom, 2016*

Right: *Sheet music for Oliver Gaggs' 'The Tower Waltz', published the year the Blackpool Tower opened in 1894*

At the turn of the twentieth century, decorum was key and young ladies were expected to be accompanied by a chaperone. A strict dress code forbade gowns that displayed too much décolletage hemlines higher than just above the ankle, and the wearing of gloves was encouraged. Young men were dressed to the nines in evening suits and highly polished shoes.

In May 1900, the Tower Company marked the end of the Boer War by offering free entrance, and over 8,000 crowded into the Ballroom – thought to be the largest ever attendance in one night.

The Edwardian period ushered in music-hall and novelty songs to the Ballroom and a less formal style of dance, of which not everybody approved. A letter to the local press from the 'Dancing Teachers of Blackpool', shortly before the outbreak of the First World War, complained of 'higgledy-piggledy' dancing, which 'would never have been permitted in father's day'.

With the advent of ragtime music in the wartime years and the Jazz Age of the 1920s came new dances from across the Atlantic, such as the Bunny Hug, the Turkey Trot and the Grizzly Bear, which swept the dance floors of the UK. Despite being declared by one outraged *Daily Mail* correspondent as 'a series of contortions', the Charleston also became hugely popular in the late 1920s – even the Prince of Wales, the future Edward VIII, was an enthusiastic and accomplished advocate of the dance. With the more modern dances came a relaxation in dress, with ankle-kissing gowns giving way to knee-length dresses.

Dances at the Tower Ballroom increased to twice daily from 1918, and by 1934, the venue's fortieth birthday, it was estimated that 100,000 people had taken a turn on the famous floor – wearing it down by five-eighths of an inch. In the post-war years, the Lindy Hop, Jive and Rock 'n' Roll took over, although the sedate Waltz remained a favourite with many of the regulars. Formal balls were also popular events, with such occasions as the Spinster's Ball and the Bachelor's Ball packing out the venue on an annual basis.

Above: *A painting by Fortunino Matania that featured in programmes for the Blackpool Tower c.1936*

Above: *A programme for the 1951 Spinster's Ball, which took place at the Blackpool Tower annually*

Above: *The* Come Dancing *judges, photographed at the Casino Ballroom in Birmingham, 1959*

Right: Come Dancing *presenter Peter West photographed during rehearsals in the studio, 1968*

Below right: *Angela Rippon as the host of* Come Dancing*, photographed in 1988*

Come Dancing

Paving the way for *Strictly Come Dancing*'s arrival on our TV screens in 2004, *Come Dancing* arrived at the Tower Ballroom in 1950. Devised by Eric Morley, the show was originally a knockout ballroom contest with teams of amateur dancers representing regions around the country, and professional dancers Syd Perkin and Edna Duffield dishing out advice. In 1953, the format changed to a competition between the four home nations – England, Scotland, Northern Ireland and Wales. The show initially ran for 45 years, until 1995, and at its height in the 1960s and 1970s it attracted audience figures of over 10 million. Regular presenters included Terry Wogan, David Jacobs and *Strictly Come Dancing* 2023 contestant Angela Rippon, who hosted from 1988 to 1991 and again on its brief return in 1998.

Above and right: *Photographs of the Blackpool Dance festival at the Empress Ballroom, 1938*

Competitions

Both the Tower Ballroom and the nearby Winter Gardens have played host to prestigious ballroom and Latin competitions for over a century, making Blackpool the dance capital of the world. Opened in 1896, the Empress Ballroom in the Winter Gardens also has a sprung floor comprised of 10,000 strips of oak, mahogany, walnut and greenwood, on top of 1,320 4-inch (10-centimetre) springs, covering some 12,500 square feet (1,160 square metres).

Since 1920, the Empress has hosted the Blackpool Dance Festival, which attracts nearly 3,000 competitors annually from over 60 countries. Spanning nine days every May, it sees dancers compete in 13 different events, and includes the British Open Championships in Adult Amateur and Professional couples, and Formation Teams. Previous winners of the Amateur Latin American crown at the festival include *Strictly Come Dancing* professional dancers Neil and Katya Jones and

Taken by the Sandman Brothers

Creative Director Jason Gilkison. *Strictly Come Dancing*'s Head Judge Shirley Ballas and former partner Corky Ballas won the Professional title in 1995 and 1996, and their son Mark Ballas was crowned Latin American Champion in 2004.

In January, the Winter Gardens hosts the Champions of Tomorrow contest, and in April, it is home to the three-day European Championships. The British National Championships, formerly known as the British Closed Championships, takes place in the Empress in November. The three-day event, which often coincides with *Strictly*'s weekend in the town, will celebrate its fiftieth anniversary in 2025.

In alternate years, the Empress also hosts the World Dance Council's (WDC) World Championship.

The Blackpool Junior Dance Festival, which has been running since 1957, was initially held in the Tower Ballroom, but in 2010 it was rehomed at the Winter Gardens. The world's biggest festival for young Latin and ballroom dancers, it incorporates the British Junior Open Championships where dancers compete in two categories: Juveniles (6 to under-12 years) and Juniors (12 to under-16 years).

Above: *Contestants in the Blackpool Junior Dance Festival, 1959*
Right: *A couple strutting their stuff at the Blackpool Dance Festival, 2023*

'The Junior Dance Festival was moved to the Winter Gardens in 2010 because their capacity is huge and the dance floor is enormous,' says Kate Shane.

'It's a beautiful ballroom, although not as ornate and as elaborate as the Tower, but, fundamentally, the Tower Ballroom was made as a visitor attraction, for people to come and dance socially, and as the competitions have evolved, it doesn't have the space the Winter Gardens has for dancers to practise, change, put on make-up, etc. A lot of the *Strictly* professionals competed here as kids, and when they arrive in the Tower Ballroom they're always buzzing because it means something to them emotionally.'

Today the Tower Ballroom's biggest competitive festival is the Open Worlds Championship. The five-day event sees champions and pro dancers from all over the globe competing in several age and genre categories, including Solo, Under-8s and the Adults' World title heats in ballroom and Latin American.

KATYA JONES, three-time World Amateur Latin Champion, is reminded of her Blackpool competitions every time she returns for *Strictly Come Dancing* and sees the British Championship hopefuls in the town. 'As a professional dancer, I love walking around town and seeing all the competitors with their hair slicked,' she says. 'It's like ballroom dancing is taking over the whole town. I love it. I bump into people I know from my dance career. It's nice to be back in my environment.'

Right: *Bertini and his band photographed at the Blackpool Tower* c.*1931*

Music Maestros

From the day its doors opened, music was an integral part of the Tower experience and, on occasion, as many as five orchestras might be playing simultaneously in the refreshment areas, dining areas and Ballroom. Legendary jazz man Duke Ellington played with his band in 1933, impressing resident saxophonist Charlie Barlow. 'Compared with them, we only toyed with our instruments,' he later recalled. 'Ellington's men really blew. We learnt a lot from that.'

A year later, the opening of the new dance floor was marked with a set from musician Larry Brennan. British composer Sir Thomas Beecham gave afternoon concerts in the Ballroom, and Dame Clara Butt also performed there. Famed jazz percussionist Eric Delaney played summer seasons at the Tower Ballroom throughout the 1980s.

Above: *Eric Delaney photographed onstage with his band at the Tower Ballroom* c.*1985*

Star turns aside, the majority of the dance music was provided by the resident dance bands, starting with the first musical director, Oliver Gaggs, in 1894, who composed the 'Tower Waltz' for the regulars at the venues. His son, Joseph Woof Gaggs, took over the Blackpool Tower Orchestra in 1905 and continued in the position for 16 years.

Throughout the 1930s, Bertini became the frontman for the Blackpool Tower Dance Band. The Londoner, whose real name was Bert Gutsell, and his 14-piece band became a national sensation through the BBC broadcasts from the Tower. His 10-year residence at the Tower saw him playing to a capacity crowd of 3,000 dancers. Bertini's fame meant that in 1936 he could leave the Ballroom and launch a national tour. That year, he and the band even featured in a film, *Dodging the Dole*. By 1937, Bertini had been replaced by Norman Newman, but many of his band members stayed on at the Ballroom, including saxophonist Charlie Barlow, who would go on to be band leader for 46 years.

There has not been a resident band since 2005, but the six resident organists provide music for the daily dancers.

Norman Newman directing the Tower Radio Band onstage at the Tower Ballroom, 1938

'A Blackpool holiday is one big party. A grand week of Punch and Judy and paper hats and streamers and dancing on the pier! One week of happiness that helps a town forget its worries and troubles.'

Singer ***Gracie Fields****, who regularly performed in the town*

Left: *Gracie Fields in Blackpool, 1967*

Blackpool Memories

Strictly Come Dancing Head Judge
SHIRLEY BALLAS

'My first memory of Blackpool was a day trip when I was six and we went to see the Blackpool Illuminations. Then I started dancing at seven and, at about nine years old, I had my first trip to the Tower Ballroom to compete. I remember my first steps in the Ballroom, walking onto the floor and just staring at the ceiling, even when the music had started. Going into a ballroom like that was so overpowering I have never forgotten it.

'The Tower Ballroom has a warmth and it is so beautifully ornate, with its red cushions and its gold trimmings, its Wurlitzer that comes up out of the stage.

'The Tower Ballroom has got the best sprung floor in the world, too, and that's not a bias but the opinion of everybody in the dance world. 'Now I can say I have competed there, I've judged competions there, I've done tea dances there and now I've been Head Judge on *Strictly Come Dancing* there too.

'These are all things that I remember from Blackpool, but everybody in the dance industry – and that's millions and millions all over the world – know Blackpool.'

Above: *Judges Shirley Ballas and Anton Du Beke dancing at the Tower Ballroom in 2022*

Fun Facts

- Originally, dancing was not permitted at the Tower Ballroom on Sundays and an evening of sacred music was performed instead.

- Rules were strict in the early days of the Ballroom and included: 'A gentleman should not dance unless he is with a lady,' and 'Disorderly behaviour means immediate expulsion.'

GOD SAVE THE KING

M.C. - - MR. W. H. PRIDGEON.

N.B.—This Programme is Subject to alteration at the discretion of the Management

No Gentleman is allowed to Dance without a Lady

Anyone Guilty of Disorderly Conduct will be immediately expelled.

- In the 1900s, alfresco dancing was a popular pastime on Blackpool's North Pier – the Blackpool Waltz and Foxtrot were favourite dances.

- Revellers in the 1920s and 1930s travelled in droves to the town on the aptly named 'Dance Trains'.

- In the 1980s, the seaside resort boasted over 75 nightclubs – more than any city in the UK.

- The ball scene for the 2021 film *Cinderella*, which starred Camila Cabello and Pierce Brosnan, was filmed in the Tower Ballroom.

- American rock band The Killers shot the video for their 2012 hit 'Here with Me' in Blackpool. Directed by Tim Burton and starring Hollywood actress Winona Ryder, the promo includes scenes in the Tower Ballroom as well as a number of locations across the resort, including the Promenade and Blackpool Pleasure Beach.

- Scenes for the 2016 Tim Burton movie *Miss Peregrine's Home for Peculiar Children* were shot in the Tower Ballroom and the Circus.

Above: *The Tiller Girls performing in the revue* Well I Never Did *at the Winter Gardens Pavilion, 1916*

The Tiller Girls

The world's longest-running dance group, the Tiller Girls, is often associated with schools in Manchester and London, but it originated in Blackpool, in 1890. Born in 1854, the troupe's founder, John Tiller, was a Lancashire cotton-mill magnate who made a fortune by the age of 25 and whose parties and entertaining were legendary among his peers. But a financial crash in his thirties left him almost penniless. Inspired by theatre shows in Manchester, where he considered the chorus girls too undisciplined in their routines, he created his own female dance group with a uniform height of around 5 feet 4 inches (1.6 metres). In teaching them synchronised routines – particularly the high-kicking line and 'pony trot' they became famous for – he is credited with inventing precision dancing.

Originally named the Four Little Sunbeams, the initial group made their first appearance at Blackpool's Pavilion Theatre and caused a sensation. With first wife Mary and later second wife Jennie, John opened and ran the Tiller School in Manchester, then another in London. By the early 1900s, he had 80 troupes around the world, with up to 32 dancers in each.

The dancers were highly trained, locking arms together onstage to perform as one, with one reviewer commenting, 'They dance as one woman, and what a woman!' – a phrase that was soon adopted as a publicity tagline.

As their fame spread, the Tiller Girls performed at the London Palladium, the Palace Theatre in Manchester and the Blackpool Winter Gardens, as well as becoming resident dancers at the famed Folies Bergère in Paris. In 1900, Tiller sent a troupe to New York, where he opened another school, and soon had three lines working on Broadway. Their success inspired the hugely successful American dance troupe the Rockettes, set up after choreographer Russell Markert saw a group called the Tiller Rockets perform in the *Ziegfeld Follies*, in

This page: *The Tiller Girls posing in their famously synchronised way, 1959*

Right: *A poster advertising a performance by the Tiller Girls, 1951*

1922. He was so impressed he decided to create his own version with 'a group of American girls who would be taller and could do really complicated tap routines and eye-high kicks', adding that 'they'd really knock your socks off'.

Most of the Tiller Girls' training took place in theatres and halls in Blackpool, where the Tillers lived and where a huge number of their protégées hailed from. Tiller only worked with untrained dancers, whom he could 'mould', and each recruit was given a rehearsal costume of a white blouse, blue shorts – which they still wear today – along with a Tiller bow tie, which they were awarded once they had passed their training. The girls would turn up to show rehearsals in their uniform, which often intimidated other performers, including the legendary Josephine Baker, who admired their high level of training.

Discipline was tight, both on and off stage. Head girls were appointed to keep order, chaperones would accompany the girls everywhere and permission had to be granted from the head office in London if they wanted to go out for the evening. They were forbidden from socialising with customers away from the show, despite many smitten fans trying to get in touch. One Tiller Girl was pursued by a French count who followed her around Europe and wrote dozens of love letters, but the pair never actually met.

In the 1900s, dancers on tour were paid £3 a week – the equivalent of £345 today – which was often more than their fathers earned. Of that, £1 went straight back to their family, £1 was kept for board and lodgings, and the remaining £1 was given to them for their expenses.

John Tiller died in 1925, but his dance troupes increased in popularity in the decades after, appearing in Hollywood movies and becoming regulars in the Royal Variety Performance and the iconic *Sunday Night at the London Palladium*.

A Tiller Girl meeting Queen Elizabeth II after a Royal Variety performance at the Winter Gardens Opera House.1955

Former Tiller Girls include Betty Boothroyd, the first female Speaker of the House of Commons, *EastEnders* star Gretchen Franklin, and Diana Vreeland, former Editor-in-Chief of *Vogue*.

Continuing Blackpool's Dance Legacy

Blackpool's association with all types of dance has recently been celebrated with the launch of a social craze, encouraging people of all ages and abilities to get dancing. The Blackpool Way was the brainchild of creatives Sam and Aishley Bell-Docherty, who teamed up with the Showtown museum and local arts organisation to come up with a routine that could be enjoyed by all, so residents could continue celebrating Blackpool's dance history.

Teacher and choreographer Sam says Blackpool holds a special place in the heart of dancers everywhere because of its rich history.

'It's a seaside town where people have come on holiday for over 100 years,' she says. 'People in the north-west regions came out of the factories and came to Blackpool to dance, especially in the days before there were so many other amusements and attractions. From the Victorians dancing on the piers and the beautiful ballrooms, to the ragtime era and later Northern Soul, it's always been a place where people have come to dance. If you speak to any ballroom dancer, wherever they are from in the world, Blackpool is iconic and often the pinnacle of their careers. But whether it's socially or competitively, it's always been a party town where people come to dance.'

In the summer of 2024, the month-long UK Capital of Dance festival once again celebrated the rich dance heritage of Blackpool, with events, dance classes and shows across the town.

Above and right: *Dancers performing The Blackpool Way, 2022*

Above: *Dancers enjoying the atmosphere at the Blackpool Mecca Ballroom, c.1965*

Northern Soul

As well as being the home of ballroom, Blackpool became one of the epicentres of Northern Soul in the late 1960s, with the Blackpool Mecca Ballroom rivalling Manchester's Twisted Wheel Club and the Wigan Casino as the go-to venue for the new craze.

Born out of the Mod scene in the UK, the music and dance movement was fuelled by DJs, including Blackpool's own Ian Levine, discovering little-known American soul tracks and B-sides, which featured a heavy beat and a fast tempo, and turning them into club anthems. During the 1960s and '70s, 3,500 people a night would dance at the Mecca Ballroom, enjoy live bands and see the introduction of Northern Soul. The Mecca, which opened in 1965, was closed down in the 1980s and later demolished.

Above: *The Blackpool Mecca Ballroom, photographed in 1978*

CHAPTER

5

Strictly Comes to Town

'I always look forward to Blackpool. It goes without saying that it is the home of dance and we love it. We always have a blast. It always feels so monumental returning home to Blackpool. We have a bigger audience than we get in the studio and we get a lovely warm northern reception, which I particularly enjoy. It's a very special week for everyone on the show.'

Tess Daly

BID ME DISCOURSE, I

HANT THINE EAR

Blackpool Week is a calendar highlight for the whole *Strictly Come Dancing* team as crew, contestants and professional dancers look forward to putting on a spectacular show in the Blackpool Tower Ballroom. But it's no mean feat to bring *Strictly* to town, and planning the move begins as early as June for the production teams. In the early summer, Production Executive Kate Jones and Executive Producer Sarah James start plotting episode dates, from the launch show and first live show onwards, factoring in the Blackpool Special in week nine of the competition. Then Kate Jones liaises with Merlin Regional Director Kate Shane and Tower Manager Kenny Mew.

'Around June, I make contact with the Tower and lock in the days that we're going to be arriving and unloading, then the real planning starts,' says Kate. 'In early September, when we're all together at the studio and I'm with the crew, we have what we call a loading meeting

Below and right: *Crew loading the camera crane, a piece of equipment that supports the camera during filming, into the Blackpool Tower*

for Blackpool and we work out how many days they need. We debrief on the year before and decide if anything needs to change to help things run more smoothly.'

Kate then works with Senior Production Manager Liane Parsley on the logistics of moving equipment 250 miles, from Elstree Studios to Blackpool, and setting up in the Ballroom ahead of the show. They come up with a detailed schedule as well as calculating how many extra crew members are needed in the week of the show. 'We have to consider things like the camera crane, which is a huge piece of equipment, and takes two hours just to carry into the building. Each department, whether it's lighting, props, cameras, etc., needs a certain number of extra crew across the week to help bring in all of the kit, and most of it has to be carried upstairs because it won't fit into the lifts.'

The magnificent props, which are bigger and bolder in Blackpool Week to reflect the space in the auditorium, have to be carefully designed to fit through the double doors leading into the Ballroom.

Scenic Supervisor Mark Osborne works with Performance Designer Catherine Land and the dance team on the props and staging for the show, and begins planning six weeks beforehand.

'The conversation always starts with: "If we had this in Blackpool, would it go through the doors?"' says Mark. 'It is an absolutely beautiful building and there's a huge staircase up to the Ballroom, but then everything has to go through one little door. We have learned, over the years, what can go in and what can't. So if anyone comes up with a huge prop I'll say, "You can have it, but it has to be in 10 pieces to fit through these doors."

'For example, Ellie Leach and Vito Coppola's huge teddy bear rack, for their 2023 Charleston, was the biggest prop we'd ever had, and that came in eight different bits and was then built in the Ballroom.

We've had some hairy moments too. Joe McFadden came down on a clock for his Salsa with Katya Jones, in 2017, and when we got the prop to the Ballroom it was too big to come through the doors. We had to get a guy to come down and literally saw the clock in half on the streets of Blackpool. But it looked brilliant on the night, and I do like it when the big props are there because it looks great on screen.'

Mark also has to consider truck space, with only one truck for the props, as well as costume, hair and make-up boxes and some of the smaller camera equipment, and four trucks for the scenery.

In total, 32 trucks are used to transport everything, from office equipment and cameras to the huge glitterballs that hang from the ornate ceiling, adding that extra *Strictly* sparkle. Travel and accommodation also has to be arranged for the cast and crew, well in advance of the November date, and Junior Production Manager Chris Mead oversees the mammoth task of making sure everyone arrives on time and has somewhere to stay.

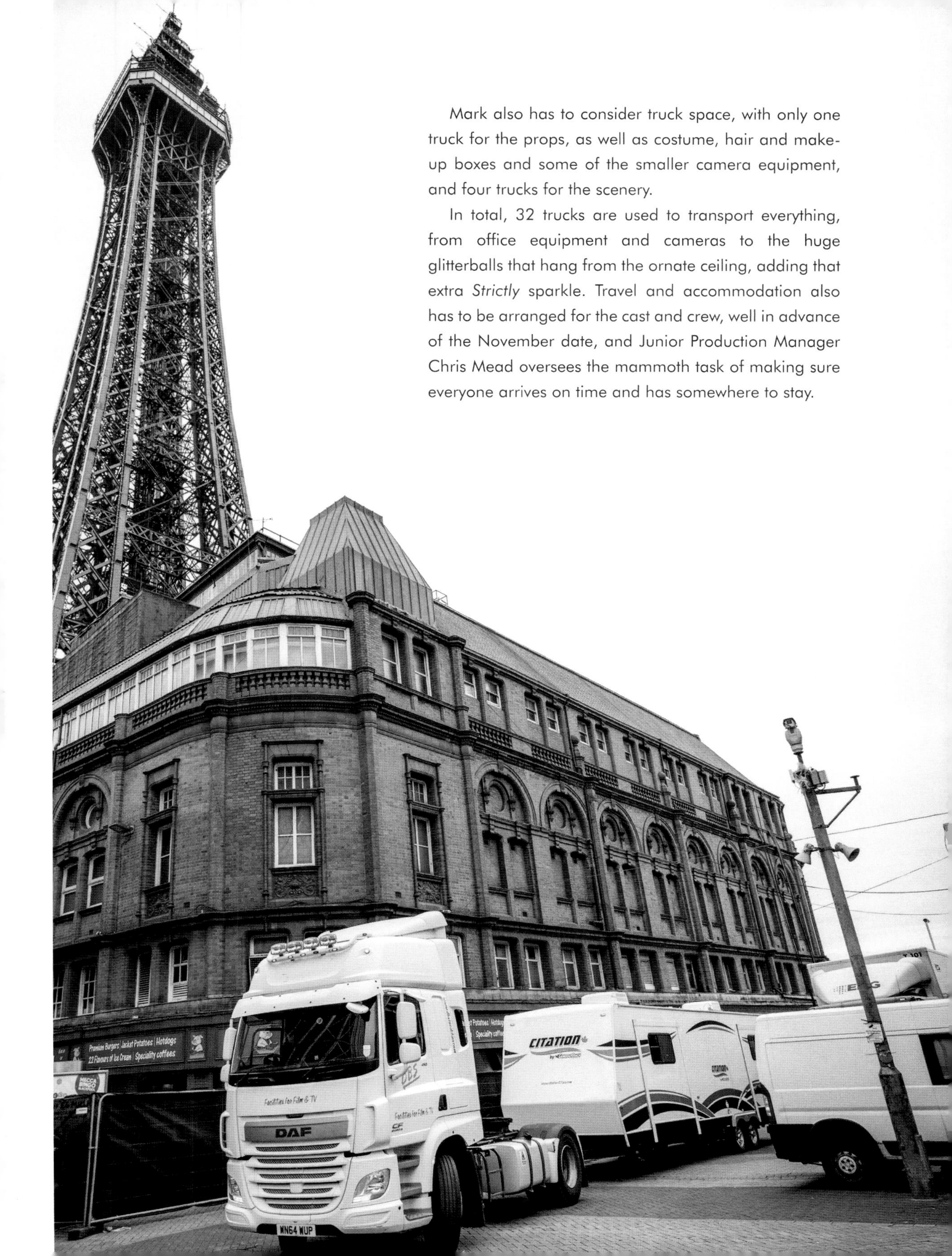

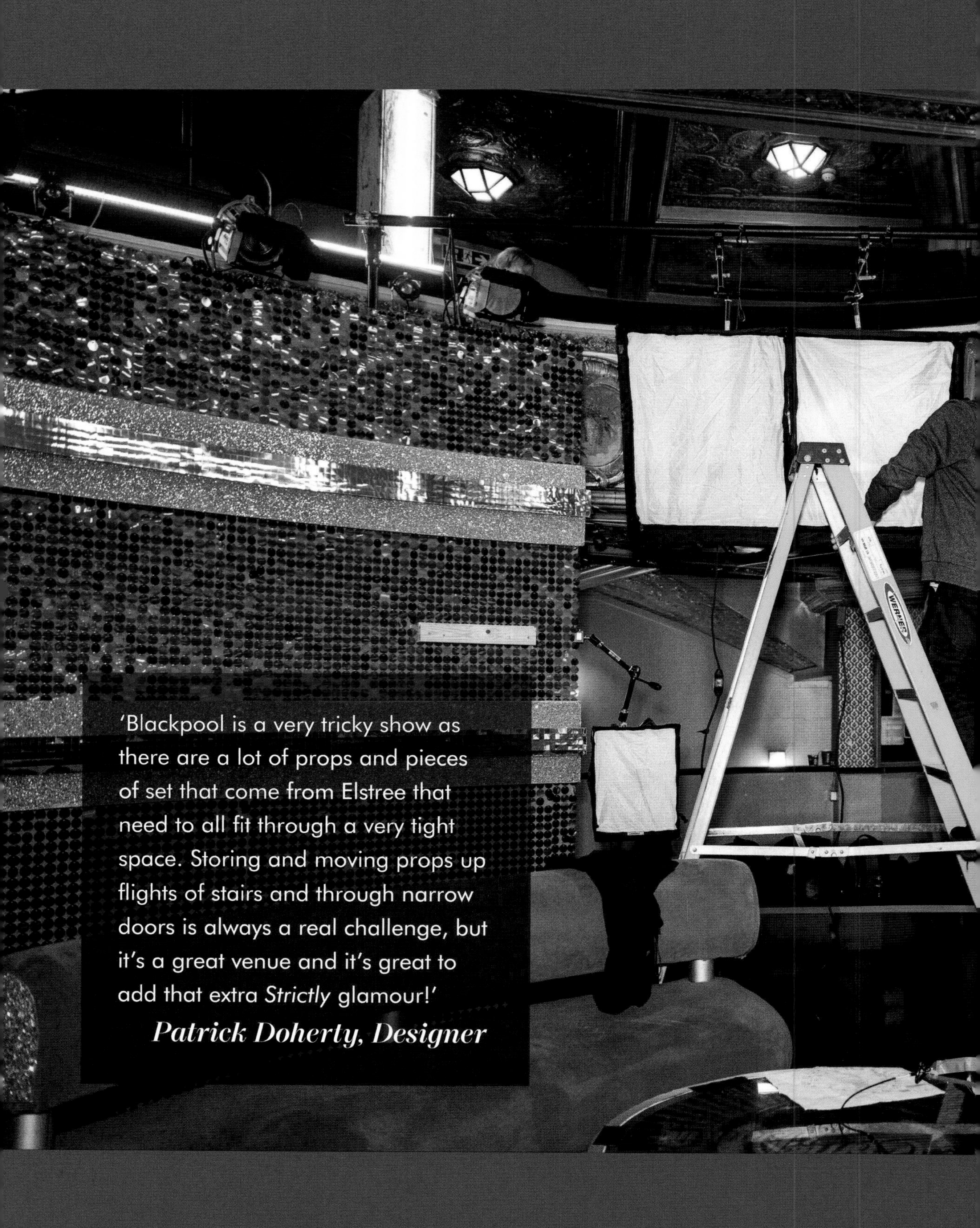

'Blackpool is a very tricky show as there are a lot of props and pieces of set that come from Elstree that need to all fit through a very tight space. Storing and moving props up flights of stairs and through narrow doors is always a real challenge, but it's a great venue and it's great to add that extra *Strictly* glamour!'

Patrick Doherty, Designer

Left: *A member of crew setting up lights in Claudia's area*

Blackpool Week

The Blackpool Special is a benchmark show for the couples and, as the weekend approaches, the excitement builds for the professional dancers and their celebrity partners.

The preparation for the move begins at Elstree Studios the Saturday before and, while the couples hone their routines in London, the *Strictly Come Dancing* production team begins moving north from Monday. It's a busy week for all involved.

SATURDAY

Elstree Studios is a hive of activity the Saturday before the Blackpool Special, as the competing couples and other professional dancers rehearse, the costume, hair and make-up teams perfect those final touches for that evening's performance and the production crew gear up for the live show. But amid the hustle and bustle, Scenic Supervisor Mark Osborne's mind is on the following week, as he allocates space in the huge articulated lorries heading to Lancashire.

'The Saturday before is when I catch up with the office team, the make-up team, the camera team and all departments,' he says. 'I just make sure they've got all their bits together and I know where they're going to leave them.'

SUNDAY

On Sunday morning Mark and his crew are back to Elstree to dismantle and collate those elements in the studio that need to be transported, including extra scenery used for the Blackpool show only, which is also stored at the Elstree base.

'We take all the furniture in the Clauditorium – the glittery background, the columns from around the set, everything which is going – and we lay it all onto the dance floor,' says Mark. 'Then I walk around, ticking everything off and taking a note of the quantity of each element, and I make sure everything is ready to be loaded onto the truck in the morning.'

The lighting alone takes three trucks, with 171 floor lights coming from Elstree and another 376 hired from an outside company.

'We have a number of different types of lights, some that do beams, some that do effects and then there are some that light the room, essentially,' says Lighting Designer David Bishop. 'The big difference in Blackpool, from my point of view, is that in Elstree, our set is self-illuminating because it's got LED product and a video wall, whereas the Blackpool Ballroom is actually extraordinarily dark. The basic rule of TV lighting is: if it's not lit, you can't see it. So even when you're looking at Tess delivering her links, and you can see the balconies in the audience, they all have to have lights pointed at them.

'The other difference is that there's no floor projection in Blackpool so we have to use a gobo, which projects patterns on the dance floor, but it's more restricted than the equipment we're able to use in Elstree.'

In Blackpool, the staff at the Tower have been prepping the backstage areas, while the tables and chairs, used for afternoon dances, are removed from the Ballroom and stored away.

Left: *Cables running out of a window, from which the glass was removed*

Right: *Members of crew carrying the camera crane upstairs and into the Ballroom*

MONDAY

The trucks are loaded at Elstree with scenery, including the judges' desk as well as costumes, make-up and hair items, lighting and riggings. Kate Jones and some of the production team are already on their way to Blackpool, ready to greet the trucks at the Tower Ballroom.

Unlike Elstree, a purpose-built studio, the Tower Ballroom was not designed for a TV production, so some adaptation is needed to make sure all the equipment and the thousands of metres of cables can be accommodated. The handrail on the main staircase to the Ballroom is removed to allow the camera crane to be carried in later in the week, and an interior window is taken out to allow cables to pass through.

'*Strictly* occupies the street at the back of the Tower, which is fenced off as a compound the whole week,' says Kate Shane. 'The crew spend two days hauling big boxes of sound and light equipment up the stairs.'

TUESDAY

It's an early start, with all hands on deck by 8 a.m. as the rig begins. A truck packed with cables from the outside broadcast (OB) company arrives and thousands of metres of cable begin to be pulled through all areas of the building.

'They load in the truss [a metal frame for lights] that the rigging team have built and it's a full day of cable and lighting rigging. It's a sea of cable everywhere you look,' says Kate Jones. 'The chandeliers that go into the ceiling also get rigged. Then the massive screen at the back of the Ballroom that holds all our graphics arrives and will start to be built, slate by slate. Behind the scenes, our runners and coordinators are setting up the rabbit warren of dressing rooms for our dancers and celebrities.'

Mark Osborne and the scenic team travel up in plenty of time to meet their truck, which arrives at the Tower at 4.30 p.m. Everything is unloaded and hauled upstairs, then laid in the correct position for construction the following day. For the next three days, an extra 16 people are drafted in and allocated to help with lighting, scenic, sound and screens, as well as the cameras, which arrive on Thursday.

WEDNESDAY

The outside broadcast or 'OB' compound, at the back of the Tower building, is coming together and Mark Osborne's team are busy building the set in the Ballroom. 'By the end of play on Wednesday, we have built the judges' area, the Clauditorium and the band area,' says Mark.

In Blackpool, judges Shirley Ballas, Craig Revel Horwood, Anton Du Beke and Motsi Mabuse sit behind a desk that was previously used in Elstree and has now been replaced with their new-look individual stations. Another difference from the Hertfordshire studio is the Clauditorium, which, by necessity, is at the side of the dance floor rather than at the top of a staircase on a different level.

Series Director Nikki Parsons arrives at the Tower on Wednesday afternoon. Part of her job is to provide a camera script, which maps out exactly which lens will be used for each shot during the live show on Saturday night and the results show.

'I begin scripting from the Monday when we go to Blackpool, starting with the group dances, because they re-rehearse the group dances on the Sunday and afterwards I am sent a wide shot of that routine,' Nikki says. 'I start seeing footage of couples' rehearsals throughout the week, so from Monday onwards right up to Friday I'm camera scripting.'

Props and scenery changes are a huge consideration for Nikki when directing cameras, so as soon as she arrives in Blackpool she gets the lowdown on how the props and staging are developing.

'I have a little walk around the Tower to check how everyone's getting on and look at any big props that have arrived, because everything's bigger and better at Blackpool, but sometimes that means they are harder to get on and off the floor and to hide from the cameras,' she says. 'It's quite a jigsaw puzzle.'

THURSDAY

The area for Dave Arch and the band is built on the stage at the back of the Ballroom, and the glitter-adorned music stands that have come up from Elstree are put in. The cameras arrive at the Ballroom and Camera Supervisor Lincoln Abraham, together with five assistants, begins to rig them up.

'The cameras that we use for the rest of the series stay in Elstree and we hire the equipment we need in Blackpool,' he says. 'So on Thursday afternoon, we take delivery of the technocrane, the huge telescopic arm, which allows us to move cameras closer and further away from the dance floor, and the biggest job is getting that up the stairs, with 16 extra men plus the camera crew all helping. The camera jib, which is placed in "the gods" on the third balcony tier and provides a lovely angle for a shot through the chandeliers, is also rigged.

4K
IMAGE STABILIZER
Canon
UHD DIGISUPER 111
UJ111×8.3B 8.3-925mm 1:1.7

Above: *Equipment in the upper balconies of the Tower Ballroom*

'In total we have 12 cameras, including the handheld Steadicam, which operator Dominic Jackson has on his arm, and he runs around the dance floor getting shots from all angles during the show. Then we've got pedestal cameras, which are on wheels, so while Claudia and Tess do their introduction, we are on the floor and when Tess introduces the first couples' dance, we move back off the floor. We have two cameras on the judges, one for close-up and one for the floor shot, and in the Clauditorium we have one trained on Claudia and two more on the professionals and celebrities.

'The only one we don't have in Blackpool, which we use in Elstree, is a rail camera, which usually sits in front of the audience, opposite the judges' desk. Because of the sprung floor, which is incredibly bouncy, it would be jigging up and down too much, so we can't use that.'

By the afternoon, the production team have all arrived and they gather for a tech planning meeting, as they do in Elstree, to talk through the logistics and details of Saturday night's show and also the concepts for the following week's show.

The scenic crew will then run through the building of the set for the opening group number and the results show group number, which can take up to 45 minutes. The various components of the set are laid out and marked out on the dance floor to make sure that they know where each piece is going, and the positions for where the competing couples stand after they've performed and are receiving their feedback from the judges is also marked out, as well as any positions for where Tess and Claudia need to stand.

Floor Manager Alan Conley, who will be making sure everything runs smoothly in the Ballroom throughout the Saturday-night show, is on hand to oversee the preparations.

Below: *Floor Manager Alan Conley and Production Designer Patrick Doherty*

'When we're in Elstree, the set is permanent and all the positions are marked on the floor,' he says. 'In Blackpool, we're literally starting from scratch again, because we have to relight all the positions, re-mark all the positions and begin the whole thing again, so that's a challenge.'

FRAGIL
event prop hire
LE24
CRYSTAL CHANDELIER-
1M DIAMETER 1.47M TALL
CONTAINS GLASS CHANDELIER - DO NOT
PORTAPROMPT
PORTAPROMPT
TRIFIBRE

Left: *An elegant glass chandelier waiting to be hung up*

The scenic team will also look at the props for the couples' dances and run through the 'setting' – how they clear the prop from one dance and create the scene for the next in the short time between routines while the video clips that introduce each dance routine are running.

'Everything's up against a really tight schedule,' says Kate Jones. 'There are only 90 seconds to "set" the props, so they can't be too complicated. But the scene setters generally have a practice if it's something that isn't as simple as just picking it up and setting it down.'

Mark Osborne has a five-man crew to help him with the quick changes, as well as a prop master, who handles the smaller items included in the dances, such as a newspaper, ice cream or cane.

'My crew and I will look at the elements for each dance and work out the best way of switching scenes in the allotted time,' says Mark. 'For instance, if two guys take one piece and three take another, then come back for something else, is that the quickest and best way? We have a practice on Thursday, so when Friday rehearsals come we're right on it and ready to go.'

While the designers try to keep it as simple as possible, liaising with Mark along the way, some sets are more complex than others. For example, in the 2023 season, Annabel Croft's beautiful American Smooth required two huge crystal chandeliers to be hung from the roof, along with flowing white drapes, which threw up a few challenges.

'You can't carry a chandelier by hand, so it has to stay in the box until it's hung,' says Mark. 'So the box had to come onto the floor, then the rigging was lowered, we hooked it on and obviously the chandelier still has to be plugged in to make it work, before it can be hoisted up, so there are a lot of elements to consider. After the dance, the chandeliers have to come down, be unhooked, unplugged and put back in the boxes.'

Mark says his favourite prop ever was for Anita Rani's Paso Doble in 2015.

'There was a huge red drape that rose from the floor and floated over the heads of the dancers as if it were flames,' he says. 'We hooked up the drape and my crew had to run along the balconies to pull it into four corners. It was a really hard thing to do and we never actually got it right until the live show, but it looked so dramatic.'

The running order is crucial to the show, especially in Blackpool, as the creative team want each dance to look as spectacular as possible. But the prop switch has to be taken into consideration when deciding which dance follows which.

'There's a carefully worked-out running order so the stage crew have got enough time to turn the scenery around, from a big piece of set to the next set,' says Series Director Nikki Parsons. 'Sometimes, you can't put two things close together. You have to take into consideration the amount of scenery you have to get on and off the dance floor.'

Storage of props in the Tower Ballroom is more challenging than in the studio at Elstree, as there are no backrooms to hide them between dances and they have to stay in the auditorium, tucked away at the sides and out of the view of the cameras.

Above: *Crew members setting up pieces of set in the Ballroom*
Right: *Anita Rani dancing the Paso Doble in front of a dramatic red drape, 2015*

'It's not like a theatre where there's a big scene dock and you can drive a lorry up and just take stuff up,' says Floor Manager Alan Conley. 'Everything has to come through a tiny little door and be built in the ballroom, and once they're put together there's no storage for the props, no wing space, and you can't store them anywhere else other than the end of the Ballroom, by the bar. You can't hide them away from the audience in the Ballroom.'

The seamless scene-shifting that the stealthy crew have perfected in Elstree is also more challenging to keep off camera in Blackpool.

'In the studio at home, the Clauditorium is up on the balcony, so when the props are being cleared, or the scenic guys are flying in, you don't see any of the staging turnaround,' explains Nikki. 'In Blackpool, because the Clauditorium is on the same level, you may be able to see bits of set being moved through the back of the shot while she's talking to the dancers. It's something we just embrace.'

Mark says the team have to practise split-second timing to make sure it all runs smoothly on the night.

'In Blackpool, we have to wait until the couple gets inside the Clauditorium to have half a chance of not getting seen. It's quite balletic in a way, in that you wait those few seconds, then as soon as the judges have given their critique, we swoop. Then, when they've given their score, we can move something else, and when the VT is on we move the rest. It really is choreography from our point of view. I've got an amazing team who are really on it.'

Once the props run is done, the lighting team go through their programme, testing the various LED lights around the Ballroom, the graphics on the big screen, and the various spotlights and coloured lights for each routine.

Right: *Dazzling lighting and video tests taking place in the Ballroom*

'At the beginning of the week, we have an idea of the concepts, the colour and the music the couples are dancing to, but we don't get the edit for the music until Tuesday or Wednesday,' says Lighting Designer David Bishop. 'So then we listen to the edits and work out what the light should be doing in terms of the music and then we look at the rehearsal tapes and work out what the light should be doing in terms of the dance. By Thursday, we have a pre-programming run to go through what we've done so we can tweak what we need to for the Friday rehearsal.'

David's department includes the graphic designers who turn the studio into a stormy sea, or a raging inferno, at the touch of a button. The technological wizardry means that even the Tower Ballroom can be transformed in the blink of an eye.

'You can manipulate size, shape and colour transition. Essentially, we take a graphic that the graphic designers come up with and we might just play that back as it arrived with us, or if a piece of music has a big drop moment or a spooky bit, we can, for example, change the colour of the graphic, so it goes with the overall lighting change.'

Backstage, the costume department are unpacking outfits, and the production team are also busy finalising set-ups and doing last-minute checks before the Friday rehearsals.

'At the end of the day, I do a full health-and-safety walk around with our Studio Resources Manager Kieran Doyle, checking every single nook and cranny on every level,' says Kate Jones. 'We go over the cabling, check the props areas, check the fire lanes are the correct width, with nothing sticking out and no trip hazards. We check that there are no sharp corners for people to catch themselves on and we'll put bubble-wrap padding around the camera platforms, and the Clauditorium, which are made up of a steel deck so they tend to have sharp corners. We check the top balconies for the sea of cabling and make sure there's enough signage and white gaffer safety-hazard tape for all of the areas and we make our full checklist.'

After a long day of frenetic activity, the lights in the Ballroom are finally switched off at around 11 p.m.

Above: *Kate Jones and David Bishop on set in the ballroom*

FRIDAY

Kate Jones does another round of safety checks, with Kieran Doyle, on Friday morning to make sure any issues flagged the night before have been dealt with before camera rehearsals get underway at 8.45 a.m.

The professional dancers, including the seven or eight extra dancers brought in for Blackpool Week, rehearse the big group numbers first, then the couples get a chance to run through their routines. 'Because the dance floor and the space are so big the whole show is supersized,' says Alan Conley. 'The props are bigger, the pyrotechnics are bigger, the effects are much bigger, plus we have the extra dancers, so we have to find time to rehearse it all.'

For the couples, who have worked hard on their routines in training studios all week, this is their first chance to try out the unique dance floor. While most of the professionals have danced on the sprung floor many times before, the bounce can come as a surprise to the celebrities when they take their first steps on it, and the scale and beauty of the building can take their breath away.

Blackpool Memories

It Takes Two Presenter FLEUR EAST

'There's a lot of hype around Blackpool and the professionals do drill into you how special and important this venue is, so when I stepped into the Ballroom for the first time, the expectations were high,' says *It Takes Two* presenter Fleur East, who danced her iconic Destiny's Child Couple's Choice with Vito Coppola in Blackpool in 2022. 'But when I walked in, even after all that hype, I was still blown away. I looked up at the ceiling and the scale of it hit me.

'Dancing on that famous dance floor was really special. I loved every moment of it. The atmosphere was electric. The energy was bouncing off the walls and I felt like the whole audience was with me and Vito in that performance. Everything that could go right on the night did. I'll never forget that experience.'

As the dancers break for lunch, Mark Osborne's team are setting up for the opening group number, which involves all the celebrities, the professional dancers and the extra dancers and, often, the four judges as well. As it's such a big number, the rehearsal lasts almost two hours. Next, Tess and Claudia, who travel to the town on Friday morning, run through their script for the following night's show.

Throughout the day the couples will also be busy filming around the town. Blackpool provides a perfect backdrop for the video clips that introduce each dance. Kate Shane, whose local knowledge is second to none, has been on hand to help in the weeks running up to the show.

'The couples might want to do something on the end of the pier or film on one of our famous trams,' says Kate. 'I know a lot of people in the town, so I help with the planning and that keeps me busy. I'm also on hand to help with anything they need in the building, and we help with security and looking after the audience.'

In the evening, the Ballroom is given over to Dave Arch and his band, for their first rehearsal in the space.

'The first time I performed in Blackpool with *Strictly* simply took my breath away. The energy in that room is electrifying. Blackpool will always be a special place for all of us dancers. The grandeur of it, the legends that have performed on that dance floor, the beauty of it – everything about it is memorable and spectacular. Blackpool will always hold a special place in my heart.'

Karen Hauer

Fun Facts

- The Clauditorium comprises 32 set pieces, plus 18 sheets of flooring and one roll of shiny covering, to provide extra sparkle.
- Sixteen columns from the Elstree studio are transported to Blackpool, to cover the marble columns in the Ballroom.
- The judges' area is made of 12 sections.
- The band area is fitted with 10 glittery music stands, which are brought from Elstree.
- It takes 16 men around two hours to carry the technocrane into the Ballroom, which is not surprising, as it weighs in at 3,300lbs (1,500kg) – roughly the weight of the average hippo or a Ford Focus car.
- There are 12 cameras in total, including four long-lens pedestal cameras, two trained on the judges, three on the Clauditorium, the Steadicam and the Jimmy jib, on the top balcony.
- It takes 547 lights to illuminate the Ballroom for the show, with 177 coming from Elstree.

CHAPTER

OURSE

ILL ENCHAN

Showtime

With excitement mounting throughout the week, and the last push to get the Blackpool Tower Ballroom ready for the live show, the big day dawns in no time. But there's still plenty to do before going live to the nation in the early evening.

Above: *A member of the costume team arranging pieces of wardrobe backstage*

SATURDAY

Lighting Designer David Bishop is among the early birds, typically arriving at 6 a.m. to get ahead of the curve before the busy day ahead.

'We come in two hours before we start rehearsing on a Saturday morning to catch up with what we've done the day before,' he says. 'The schedule is tight and we're tweaking throughout.'

The Tower building begins to fill up at 8 a.m., with the professionals and celebrity dancers arriving for hair, make-up and costume, and production staff gearing up for the live show. In the Ballroom, the band is in place ready to play for the couples, who are each given two runs of their routines throughout the morning.

After lunch, the guest musical act is rehearsed, then it's time for the all-important dress rehearsal, where the whole show comes together for the first time. Together with the band run in the morning, the couples rehearse on the Tower Ballroom dance floor six times before the live performance, in order to get used to the sprung floor.

Above and left: *Dancers enjoying final rehearsals for the group numbers*

'The sprung floor has its own challenges because some of the cameras bounce, the judges' desk bounces and everything in the room bounces,' say Alan Conley. 'It also means the dancers travel further. You can adjust the floor to different types of dances, depending on what's in the Ballroom. There's a panel in the middle of the floor, which they can take out and underneath is a mechanism that they turn to make it more or less bouncy, which is brilliant.'

The beautiful retractable glass roof, so treasured by dancers over the years, also provides a challenge for the production team.

'I love the fact that the roof is retractable, but because it's glass it means the sunlight comes through and affects the lights,' explains Alan. 'So we have black tarpaulin on the roof to cover that up, to stop the light getting through.'

After the dress run, all the different departments will liaise with Executive Producer Sarah James, Production Executive Kate Jones, Series Director Nikki Parsons and the production team on any last-minute changes needed to make the show as spectacular as possible.

'Even after the dress rehearsal we're still making changes, all the way up until the video clip that runs as the couples walk on,' says Lighting Designer David Bishop. 'We put every dance together, effectively, in 20 minutes, because that's all the rehearsal time we have, so we are right up to the wire almost every single time.'

While the cast break for an early dinner, the audience are seated and legendary warm-up man Stuart Holdham keeps them entertained as the crew set up for more group dance rehearsals before the live show.

Crowd Pleaser

The arrival of *Strictly Come Dancing* in the seaside town of Blackpool causes quite a buzz among both the locals and the many dancers visiting for the Blackpool Dance Festival at the Winter Gardens. The Blackpool illuminations are kept on for the occasion, and even the shop displays reflect the glamour of the event, with gold and silver jackets and sparkly dresses often glittering in the windows.

Behind the Tower Ballroom building, crowds begin to gather on Friday and numbers swell on Saturday, with *Strictly* superfans willing to brave all weathers to catch a glimpse of their favourite judge, professional dancer or celebrity.

'The town is absolutely buzzing and when we arrive at the Ballroom there will be a crowd outside trying to get autographs or pictures with everyone,' says Camera Supervisor Lincoln Abraham. 'They absolutely love the show coming up there. It is a fantastic atmosphere.'

Locals Ann Moulding and Wendy Nickson are among the diehards who join fellow fans at the stage door on the day, and they say the show brings some sparkle to the town.

'It's very exciting,' says Ann. 'It brings revenue to the town and it's nice for us, as locals, to come and see the stars in the flesh.'

Above left and right: *Fans lining the street outside the Blackpool Tower to catch a glimpse of the stars of* Strictly Come Dancing

Ann's friend Wendy is also a devoted fan. Speaking outside the Ballroom, she said: 'You really want to see your favourites in real life when they come to Blackpool. I came last night because I wanted to know what was going on. I've been watching the show from the start. I absolutely love it.'

Adele Clayton and daughter Ayla, 13, were also hoping to catch a glimpse of the stars outside the Ballroom. 'It brings so much fun and enjoyment to people, when *Strictly* is here,' says Adele. 'It's just the buzz. Everybody comes out to see it.'

Ayla has been watching the show since she was a little girl and the pair also love the Live Tour, travelling to Manchester to see the couples in action. 'We love all the make-up and the costumes, as well as the dancing. It just makes us smile all the time,' says Adele.

Sonia and Steve Marshall, from Warwickshire, travelled to Blackpool for the Dance Festival, with daughter Harriet, who was competing, and younger daughter Brie. The whole family are also fans of *Strictly Come Dancing* and, while in town, they joined the crowds outside the Ballroom.

'The girls love the dresses and we all love the dances,' says Steve.

Sonia reveals how the show has inspired Harriet. '*Strictly* has helped show her how to extend and fully execute all the moves and smile – since she's been watching *Strictly* she's got it!'

Live Show

When the famous theme tune kicks in, and Tess Daly and Claudia Winkleman appear on the dance floor, the excited audience is ready to raise the elaborate roof. The Tower Ballroom has seating for even more people than the studio in Elstree, meaning the atmosphere cranks up a notch.

'Blackpool is an extension of the show, and it feels very natural to be in the Ballroom,' says Floor Manager Alan Conley. 'It enhances the whole series for me and it's my favourite episode. I love the way it looks and the way it feels, and having that bigger audience creates an even bigger atmosphere. The space allows a lot more *Strictly* fans to come and they get really excited by it.'

When creating her camera script, Series Director Nikki Parsons makes sure the grandeur of the Ballroom can be experienced by the viewers at home, with a favourite view being the long shot from the third balcony, through the chandelier, as the light glints off the mirror balls hanging from the roof.

'The Ballroom always looks beautiful on camera,' says Nikki, 'because you've got the balconies, the beautiful plasterwork and the architecture. It's a lovely place to shoot. I love the challenge of it, and it's so much fun. It's at a really good point in the series, just over midway, and it's something to look forward to, which is a big spectacular. Also, the audience reaction in Blackpool is amazing.'

'My favourite shot every year is the one from the huge crane camera that they've got set up on the furthest point at the top. It shoots through the chandelier and you see the entire Ballroom from this high perspective and it looks so magical. It's such an amazing space.' *Janette Manrara*

For the professional dancers, the Blackpool show is a homecoming, and the whole cast throw themselves into the show with renewed enthusiasm, determined to put on an extra-special show for the audience in the auditorium and at home.

'Blackpool Week is absolutely wonderful because of the electrifying atmosphere,' says Craig Revel Horwood. 'It's one of the things that the celebrities look forward to, because if they make it to Blackpool, they feel like they've achieved something, so that's a major goal. After that, we know who has a chance to make it into the Final and the battle is well and truly on. It's a good benchmark and it's fun because it's an achievement, I think, that everyone celebrates.'

Taking to the Floor

With seven couples' routines, two huge group numbers and the musical act, Creative Director Jason Gilkison has his work cut out, but he's always a few steps ahead, nailing down some of the professional routines as early as August. Series Director Nikki Parsons is briefed on these group routines in the summer and, as the Blackpool date approaches, she'll be across the proposed props, lighting, graphics and staging as well as the dance content.

'We keep Blackpool in mind throughout the entire season and we have a clear idea of the shape of the show long before we know which couples are dancing,' says Jason. 'We put the music and ideas together for the group numbers in May and rehearse the skeleton of them in August. The Blackpool opening number, which I choreograph, is a bit more difficult than the results-show professional routine because it includes the remaining celebrities. The first time we rehearse, we don't even know who the celebrities for the series are, let alone who will be in the final seven and therefore performing at Blackpool. You have no idea of what they can do. We also don't know which professionals are still going to be in the competition, so we try to come up with something we can shift around.

'The weekend before Blackpool we do another rehearsal, when we actually know who the "Magnificent Seven" are going to be.'

As well as the professionals and celebrities, and often the four judges, the group dances incorporate the extra dancers, who also join the Sunday rehearsal.

'The extra dancers are also involved in the couples' dances, so sometimes it feels like there are 10 group dances in the show,' says Jason. 'But they pick up choreography quickly because they're professional dancers at the top of their game, so they're really on the ball. They come in with a fresh energy, which is great.'

For the couples' dances, it's only two weeks before the Blackpool show that the dance concepts begin to be plotted in earnest.

'We want to make sure each couple has something really exciting for Blackpool,' says Jason. 'Dances like the American Smooth, Waltz, Quickstep, Charleston, or an Argentine Tango or a Paso Doble look really dramatic on that floor. So in the forward planning, we make sure we can give the celebrities something they feel they could really deliver at Blackpool. We are also thinking about the opportunities to work in extra dancers, what props we can build for them and so on.'

During the rest of the series, the couples rehearse close to the celebrity's home or work base, wherever that may be in the country. But in the week before the Blackpool show, all the couples stay in London for one extra night after the show so they can rehearse the Blackpool group number on Sunday.

'After the previous week's show, they have the group rehearsal bright and early the next morning, then the couples scatter to rehearse their routines as usual. We head up to Blackpool on Thursday so they can all rehearse in the Ballroom on Friday.'

As a former competitor in Blackpool himself, Jason is a huge fan of the sprung floor in the Ballroom. 'It's great for the dancers to dance on the incredible sprung floor, which is the best in the world,' he says. 'It is really good for their legs and really helps their recovery, particularly if they're doing numbers with lots of jumping, like the Charleston or Jive.'

Even as the couples rehearse their routines, Jason and the rest of the teams are finalising the running order, but Jason says Mark Osborne and the props team play a huge part in deciding the show's final running order.

'Our prop boys are magnificent,' he says. 'The ons and offs are just amazing, and I don't know how they do it, to be honest. There's no storage in Blackpool, so the props are all piled up on top of each other down in the corridor, and the way they are able to make it happen during a live show dictates the order. So we're in the hands of the props team. If needed, they may say, "These two can't follow each other because we're never going to get it on and off in time."'

Above: *Angela Rippon and Kai Widdrington dancing the American Smooth in the 2023 Blackpool Special*

Left: *The spectacular biggest-ever* Strictly Come Dancing *group routine taking place at the Tower Ballroom in 2013*

Jason has been choreographing group numbers at Blackpool since 2013 and his favourite group routine at the venue is still the first one he created, to Candi Staton's 'Young Hearts Run Free'.

'We had a lot of people from outside the *Strictly* bubble, including about 40 older ballroom dancers and a lot of kids. It was a number which showed how inclusive ballroom dancing could be and I think that was one of my best memories there. I also loved 2022's musical-act dance to 'You're the Voice' with Sam Ryder, which was based around Amy Dowden and included a nine-year-old Amy, played by Pebble-Rose Spratt, and a young Kai Widdrington, played by Luca Ivanets. That was so moving.

'Every year, I actually get really excited about the Blackpool number. It's one of my favourites to work on.'

As a former ballroom and Latin champion himself, Jason thinks Blackpool and *Strictly Come Dancing* are a perfect fit. 'As long as Blackpool is the spiritual home of ballroom dancing, we need to do a Blackpool episode. It's a standalone themed week for us and you never get over hearing what they call the "Blackpool roar" – the sound of the audience, which shakes your bones when you're in that room.'

'My first job in this country was in *Cats*, in 1989, and I was playing the Winter Gardens, which was also the first time I saw the Blackpool Tower and the Ballroom. I fell in love with it. I had just come from Paris and I'd been living near the Eiffel Tower. The Blackpool Tower looked like the top of that. I also remember having to put 50p in the meter for electricity in the digs where I was staying. I'd never done that before! One of my fondest memories of Blackpool is the launch of my Madame Tussauds waxwork, in 2018. We held it in the Ballroom and my waxwork had six showgirls dancing around it, which was fun.'

Craig Revel Horwood

Above: *Musical Director Dave Arch poised at the piano in the Tower Ballroom*

A Musical Interlude

The rich history of dance in the Tower Ballroom goes hand in hand with musical acts, whose notes have reverberated through the rafters since 1894. For *Strictly*'s Musical Director Dave Arch, the orchestra and the singers, Blackpool Week offers a chance to play in an iconic venue, purpose-built for big bands and orchestras, and with very different acoustics to the TV studio.

'Like any change of venue it takes a little while to acclimatise to the sound,' says Dave. 'We go from a studio in London to a very big, ambient room. If you drop a pin in silence, it rings around the room, so every drumbeat reverberates through the whole building.'

The process of writing the arrangements for the tracks remains the same as any other *Strictly* week. As soon as the couples lock in their choices, Dave works with Music Producer Ian Masterson to recreate each track in the 90-second format required for the couples' routines. Ian produces a version for the couples to use in rehearsal and Dave writes the arrangement for the live band to play on Saturday night.

'The writing process is the same, but we take the different acoustics into account when we mix it all together,' says Dave. 'With some tracks in the studio, for example, we put false reverberation in to make it sound as though it's in a big room. So when we have the big Ballroom, we use less.'

Just as the Blackpool dance floor works well for spectacular and dramatic dances, the capacious auditorium is perfect for the big-band sound, and Dave says classic tracks work best.

'It's a fantastic room for what I call traditional dance music, like big-band music and the older-style tunes,' he says. 'It's a flagship show so we always want to put on the most spectacular dances, and we want the music to be as impressive as we can make it. But the big-band numbers sound fantastic in the Ballroom and the professionals often comment on how good that sound is to dance to. It moves a lot of air.'

The orchestra's kit from Elstree is shipped up early in the week, with Dave, the 15-strong orchestra and the four singers arriving on Friday. The first time they go through the tracks together is at band rehearsal on Friday night and they will be at their music stands early on Saturday morning for the group and couples' rehearsals, when the live music and routines come together for the first time.

'The Friday-night rehearsal takes a bit longer than usual to get going because it's in a new venue with a new sound,' he says. 'Also, a lot of the musicians have to be further away from me because, rather than the small square section we have in Elstree, we have a long, narrow rectangle, to fill the stage. We need to adjust to a different sound, but it's very rewarding.'

Dave's first foray into the grand Ballroom was in 2009, three years after he took up his place at the head of the *Strictly Come Dancing* orchestra.

'It's a beautiful building and you can feel all that history there,' he says. 'The Blackpool shows are always very special because the audience is louder and more prominent, so all of the shows we have done there have been really atmospheric.'

Above: *The* Strictly Come Dancing *orchestra performing for a group number during the Blackpool Special in 2016*

Leaving Town

When the last dance is danced, and the cameras have stopped rolling, the dancers, celebrities, judges and presenters head back to the hotel. But the hard work isn't over for Scenic Supervisor Mark Osborne, Camera Supervisor Lincoln Abraham and the rest of the crew. The cameras and sound equipment have to be derigged and the props dismantled, ready to be loaded out.

The following day the loading-out work continues, with lighting, screens and other scenery elements also being removed.

'We load between four and five trucks in about three and a half hours,' says Mark. 'That's when Kate Jones calls me "head of pointing", because I never touch anything. There are so many men there, so I stand and point, saying, "That goes on the white truck, blue truck, green truck."'

For some, the clearing of the Tower building can spill over to the following day as well, with the weather affecting one team in particular. 'The rigging team have a really hard job because if the winds are really high, they can't then get up in the roof for health and safety reasons so they can't de-rig the main truss,' says Kate Jones.

Blackpool Memories

It Takes Two Presenter JANETTE MANRARA

Janette Manrara danced as a *Strictly* professional from 2013 until 2020, and took celebrity partners Jake Wood and Peter Andre to the dance floor in the Tower Ballroom.

'The Blackpool weekend is my favourite of the whole series,' she says. 'Out of all the themed weeks, I think it's the most special because it's the most iconic place to dance. It always landed near my birthday, so I always felt like Blackpool was a celebration just for me. I never competed there, but I remember when I first walked into the Ballroom, I felt the history, I felt all the championships. Aljaž [Škorjanec] was telling me his stories about how he was going to Blackpool since he was five years old, and all the professionals talked about how they competed. When I did my first dance there it was with *Strictly Come Dancing*. The energy in the room when you walk in to dance on that dance floor, every single year, felt special. There is something in the air when you're in that ballroom that you just can't explain. I felt it massively when I was a part of it with *Strictly*.'

By Monday, Mark is back at Elstree and once more greeting the trucks that bring the show back to the studio and making sure everything that was taken to Blackpool is reinstated in time for the following Saturday's show.

Mark has been involved in moving the show to Blackpool since 2009 and says he has fond memories of the shows there.

'The first year I went with *Strictly*, I'd never been to Blackpool before,' he recalls. 'I just looked at it and I thought, "Wow." I was blown away by how ornate it is. When you compare it to a lot of architecture now, and think how long ago that building was built and how beautiful it is, it's incredible. I fell in love with it.'

Right: *Janette Manrara and Peter Andre performing during the Blackpool Special in 2015*

CHAPTER

7

Getting the Look

When it comes to the wardrobe, Costume Designer Vicky Gill adds her special magic to each and every routine for the Blackpool extravaganza. Although Blackpool is on her mind through the whole series, Vicky and her team start to pull together ideas just 10 to 12 days before the Blackpool Special.

'After doing the show for a number of years, I'm always plotting in my head how we can make Blackpool work,' says Vicky. 'But in terms of concepts, once we know who is in the show, that's when everybody really starts to focus. It's really in the final couple of weeks before the show that the stars align.'

With the group and couples' dances, and the extra professionals, Vicky and her team are tasked with coming up with 104 looks for the *Strictly Come Dancing* Blackpool Special. But, knowing that nothing is set in stone until the camera is rolling, Vicky plans for over 300, in case of last-minute changes. In the week before the move, each garment is packed away as it's completed, with Wednesday being the final day to get everything together before the wardrobe van collects it all from Elstree early on Thursday morning.

'On average, we have three looks for every one person per dance because you never know what might change,' she says. 'In Elstree, we have stock or we might nip into London to buy extras, but in Blackpool, there isn't time to run out to grab last-minute additions.'

As well as the costumes, the wardrobe team transport steaming equipment to look after the costumes as well as a spin dryer, which helps if a garment needs to be dried on site. The wardrobe team also bring seven sewing machines, in addition to their entire stock of sequins and stones for that much-loved sparkle.

Above: *A crew member unloading costumes at the Blackpool Tower*

Below: *A member of the costume team steaming a garment backstage*

Above: *Sparkly stones being prepared for application to the dancers' glamorous costumes*

Left: *A wardrobe rail of fabulous costumes backstage at the Blackpool Tower*

'If something's very heavily embellished, we might need a minimum of 10 packets of sequins, so we take as many as we can,' she says. 'We have five seamers who all have their own sewing machines, and we also take a couple of spare machines because we always need back-up.'

Vicky's team will always need to make changes once the routine comes together and the costumes are seen on the dance floor for the first time.

'Until you see the routine in situ, on the screens, it's difficult to know what works and what doesn't. The minute that we see it on the dance floor, in the dress run, we know if a colour is missing or something else needs to be changed.'

Costume fittings take place throughout Friday and Saturday, with professionals and celebrities popping in to have jackets altered, dresses sewn and embellishments added. Even after the dress rehearsal, on Saturday afternoon, there will be plenty for the wardrobe department to do, altering

On this page: *Busy members of the costume team planning and preparing the dancers' costumes*

the fit, sewing up hems or gluing on hundreds of stones. 'We're working right up to the next camera call,' says Vicky. 'We look at the filming schedule and prioritise, so alterations for the results show will be done during the main live show.'

During the live broadcast, some of Vicky's team will be making last-minute alterations, while others are in the quick-change area to help the performers with the three-minute turnaround in the dances, and ready to deal with any costume issues that crop up.

Vicky, who has been running wardrobe for 11 years, says Blackpool is lots of work but rewarding for all. 'We always have a good time. The effort and the application is second to none, because we're all there to do a job; there are no distractions because we're away from home and we all give it 150 per cent.'

'People often ask me about a favourite costume, but I get most excited when the whole number is great,' Vicky continues. 'One of my favourites was the opening number with Gloria Estefan, in 2018. We had the girls in feathered headdresses and the boys in white and black; it was all very clean, and she was fabulous. It's that moment when you just think, "Everything is just great – good job, everybody." That's what I most remember because, with *Strictly*, it's all the elements of the production that make it fabulous: the lighting, band, set design and so on. Moments like that are my favourite memories, rather than the garments themselves.'

'Every time you walk into the Ballroom and look up, you just imagine all the events that happen in there and, back through time, all the joy and the many emotions that have happened within that space. That's what always gets me. When we're there as a production, and the band fires up, and you see the sprung dance floor, there are many little elements that make it feel special and different. You embrace the whole dance world and you're immersed in that entertainment.'

Vicky Gill

Above: *Costume Designer Vicky Gill*
Right: *Head of Makeup and Hair Design Lisa Armstrong*

Fun Facts

- Wardrobe take approximately 300 packets of crystals to Blackpool to stone the clothes. With 1,140 in each packet, that's 342,000 stones.
- One garment could take 10 packets – or 11,400 stones – to embellish.

Completing the look for each dance is the job of hair and make-up, whose wizardry can transform an elegant ballroom look into a quirky 1920s Charleston style in an instant. The weekend before the Blackpool show Lisa Armstrong, Head of Make-up and Hair Design, and Hair Designer Lisa Davey will make sure all the products and equipment they need are packed up and ready to travel to Blackpool in the props lorry.

'We have to make sure we've remembered everything, so for the hair team, we have boxes and boxes of wigs, hair pieces and accessories,' says Lisa Armstrong. 'Then we have make-up, lashes, tan, nail varnish, setting sprays and so on. Between us we send 16 boxes, and then the team also bring their own kit with them.'

Before packing up what they need on the Saturday before the show, the hair and make-up team are given a concept document, which captures the mood of the dance, and colour suggestions, so they can get a idea of what they need to take. But knowing anything can change over the next week, they pack for all eventualities.

'We take up hair pieces, ponytails and everything that we know we will definitely need, then we put in extras like hair bling, accessories, all the hair and wigs,' says Lisa Davey. 'It all takes up about six big boxes, and then there's my kit, as well as hairdryers, tongs, etc.'

The two Lisas work on the designs for the couples' dances through the week before, after finding out which couples remain in the contest

and what their dances are. They consult with Vicky in the costume team on styles and colour schemes and come up with sketches and palettes by the Thursday before the Blackpool Special. These are tweaked on Friday, when the rehearsals and costume fittings are underway.

'Blackpool is such a big show in the *Strictly* calendar, because it's the home of dance so everyone wants a chance to perform at the Tower Ballroom,' says Lisa Armstrong. 'As a show, we want to make it spectacular.'

With the extra dancers performing in both the group and couples' numbers, speed is of the essence when changing a look. 'We have to factor in all the dancers' quick changes, because they might have one number where they're doing a Waltz in classic ballroom style and then they might be involved in the Jive with the next couple, but you only have a three-minute change,' she says. 'In that time we may have to go from a bun to a pony tail, change a soft lip into a red lip, all while they're changing clothes in a tiny backstage area, before getting them back onstage.'

When considering the styles she can quickly switch up, Lisa Davey has an arsenal of clever ideas, accessories and hair pieces on hand for an instant change.

'After the opening dance, the couples have to change back into the competing looks for the main show and the extra dancers are going from one dance to another. I have to work out the quickest thing we can do so that they blend in with each dance,' she explains. 'Sometimes we can only change the hair slightly or take an accessory out, because we don't have much time.'

Overall, a dancer could need six different looks over the course of the Blackpool Special, which, factoring in the dress rehearsal before the live show, means 12 changes on a Saturday.

'The schedule is meticulously worked out because everybody needs to know where everybody is at any one time,' says Lisa Armstrong. 'The dancers have to rehearse with the live band in the morning, and we have to be very conscious of people getting enough time with each department. So if we have someone for an hour, we have to make sure we stick to that so they don't lose time with wardrobe or in rehearsal.'

For Blackpool Week, both hair and make-up have seven stylists and two assistants each. On the day of the show, the performers are in the stylists' chair early in the morning, and a steady stream will come through their door all day.

Right: *A view of the busy makeup room upstairs in the Blackpool Tower*

'There's a lot involved in getting everyone finished on time for the show,' says Lisa Davey. 'People often think the dancers turn up at 5 p.m., get their hair done, then go out on the dance floor, but some are in the chair from the 8 a.m. slot, and they'll keep coming back all day.'

The Saturday dress rehearsal is the first chance to truly test the quick changes, working with wardrobe to see if the process needs further tweaking.

'We have four hair and make-up stylists in the quick-change area, some over the other side of the Ballroom to check the couples as they enter, and one with Anton Du Beke and Craig Revel Horwood. Then we have a smaller group in the make-up room in case of any last-minute bits and pieces,' says Lisa Armstrong.

'For the dress run, it's all about timings. If we haven't got time to change even just the hair and the lipstick between dances, then it can't be done. The executive producer will also send notes afterwards for other small changes we need to make.'

As the show goes live, the make-up and hair departments are at full pelt until the last credits roll, but the backstage camaraderie means there's plenty of fun. 'We're all like a little family and it feels like a holiday for a couple of days,' says Lisa Armstrong. 'I always love going to Blackpool.'

Lisa, who has worked on the show since 2007, remembers dancing in Blackpool's Winter Gardens as a child and says she still loves coming back to the town.

'I get excited about going to Blackpool because, when you're there in the Ballroom surrounded by beauty, with the excitement of the audience, and the band kick off, it's magical. It's the home of ballroom and Latin, so it's a special place to go. I still get goose bumps every time I walk in.'

Blackpool Memories

Strictly Professional LUBA MUSHTUK

Luba Mushtuk, a four-time winner of the Italian Dance Championship and an Italian Open Latin Show Dance Champion, remembers dancing in Blackpool from the age of 10.

'Blackpool has a big place in my heart because I've been dancing there since I was a tiny little girl. When I first started dancing it was this magical place that I used to dream about, because our teacher was always saying, "Once you are ready, once you get better, we will go to Blackpool." When we were finally ready, it was a huge achievement to me to be there at all.

'The first time I danced there was in the Junior Championships, when I was 10, and we were in the final, finishing in third place. I was over the moon!

'It was a very special place from the start. Once you walk in, you can't actually explain it, but there is something in the air in the Tower Ballroom. Its art is in the air. I don't know what it is but I feel it in my skin, I can smell it, and it's just so beautiful.'

CHAPTER

Backstage in the Ballroom

'I absolutely love Blackpool Week. We get so excited. We're like schoolkids. I eat an awful lot of rock and we get fish and chips from a local chip shop. The Tower Ballroom is extraordinary. When you walk in it's so beautiful, overwhelming. The town is always so welcoming to us as well. It's absolutely one of my favourite weekends.'

Claudia Winkleman

While the beauty and majesty of the Tower Ballroom is transformed into a temporary TV set for the weekend, the rest of the vast building becomes the backstage area, with dressing rooms for performers and hosts, a production office, hair and make-up rooms and a whole host of production staff vying for space. The 130-year-old Tower building is a maze of corridors leading to tiny cubby-holes and odd-shaped rooms, which are adapted for use by the ingenious *Strictly Come Dancing* crew.

MONS

'It is a very different environment and we are working with a lot less space,' says Production Executive Kate Jones. 'The dressing rooms are very different to Elstree, and other than Tess Daly and Claudia Winkleman, who also have tiny spaces, nobody gets an individual dressing room.'

Unlike in Elstree, the physiotherapy area is not a dedicated room, but an area on the ground floor, which is usually an amusement arcade.

'We have to set up makeshift physio areas in a section of the arcade,' says Kate. 'We put up pipe and drape cubicles, so the physio beds are divided with a drape either side, and we put in a portable heater, and everyone just gets on with it.'

Because of the lack of dressing room space inside, the four judges are housed in individual trailers, parked in a compound outside the back door of the Tower building. A fenced-off area, in the midst of a busy shopping street, is also host to production portacabins, which double for Elstree's gallery, with directors, sound and lighting crew overseeing the show from outside the back door.

'Our portacabins and trailers arrive on Wednesday morning, then they are loaded into the compound and carefully configured,' says Kate. 'It's quite an operation to get everything into the right place, because if one is a couple of feet out, it just doesn't fit. Our Studio Resources Manager Kieran Doyle makes sure everything's in exactly the right place to make it all work, and the fencing goes up.'

Lighting Designer David Bishop is among the crew that spend the majority of the week in the outside trucks, in the remote control room. 'In the days before I took over, we used to sit inside the Ballroom, but now we've moved to a portacabin by the trucks, which works really well. On the night of the show the gaffer and sparks will be inside, along with seven spotlight operators, but everyone else is outside.'

Above: *The remote control room, situated in a porta-cabin outside the Blackpool tower*

Being in the outside compound means David gets in plenty of steps during Friday and Saturday.

'It's a beautiful ballroom but the thing that always sticks with me is the stairs, because there are so many,' he says. 'I need to be on the studio floor as well as in the control room quite a lot, so I end up sprinting up and down three flights of stairs dozens of times a day!'

Blackpool Memories

Strictly Professional MICHELLE TSIAKKAS

Michelle Tsiakkas's first Blackpool experience was in an adult competition in the Winter Gardens, in 2019. She has danced with *Strictly* in the Tower Ballroom since 2022. 'I grew up in Cyprus, so I competed there and in some international competition but sadly never Blackpool,' she says. 'Dancing in the Winter Gardens was really special but different from the Tower, which is more intimate. The actual space in the Ballroom is mind-blowing. It's also really hard to navigate yourself around the building. I always get lost, even though I have been there before.'

DIO$ NOS
DEL

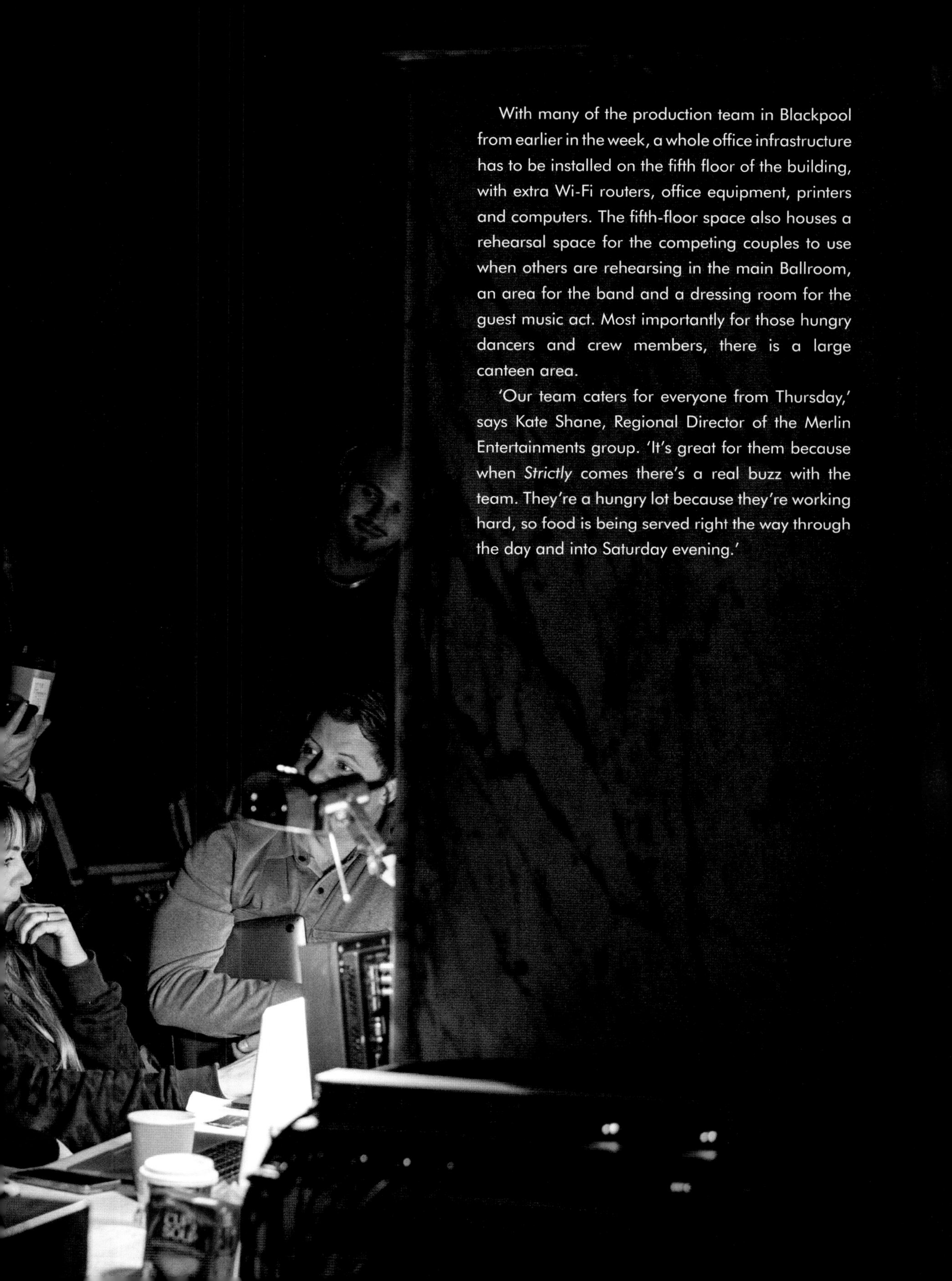

With many of the production team in Blackpool from earlier in the week, a whole office infrastructure has to be installed on the fifth floor of the building, with extra Wi-Fi routers, office equipment, printers and computers. The fifth-floor space also houses a rehearsal space for the competing couples to use when others are rehearsing in the main Ballroom, an area for the band and a dressing room for the guest music act. Most importantly for those hungry dancers and crew members, there is a large canteen area.

'Our team caters for everyone from Thursday,' says Kate Shane, Regional Director of the Merlin Entertainments group. 'It's great for them because when *Strictly* comes there's a real buzz with the team. They're a hungry lot because they're working hard, so food is being served right the way through the day and into Saturday evening.'

On the third level, where the main Ballroom sits, the surrounding corridors are a mass of wires and technical equipment. In a backstage area dubbed Penny Lane, as it used to house the Penny Arcade, boxes are lined up against the stunning decorative walls, which reflect the magnificent decor in the Ballroom. 'This is now back of house, but in the early days of the Ballroom it wasn't,' says Kate Shane. 'So the beautiful decor continues in areas like these, which very few people ever see.'

Below: *Trunks of equipment lining the passageways backstage at the Blackpool Tower*

Above: *The costume team working on dresses for the show*

Up a flight of wide stairs, another surprisingly narrow, uneven and twisty staircase leads to the bustling costume department, situated in the rafters of the building. At the back of the room, another storage area is host to rails and rails of amazing outfits, with sparkly dresses, stone-studded jackets and sequinned tops making the tiny area into an Aladdin's cave of fabulous dancewear.

'Wardrobe is in a narrow attic room,' says Vicky Gill. 'But it's an old building, so it's what you'd expect, and those walls tell so many stories. We make it work as a space. There is a surface that runs around the perimeter, and we put tables anywhere we feel that we can fit one.'

Being at the top of the building and several flights of stairs away from the doors where the trucks load and unload means Vicky and her team are one step ahead when it comes to moving the costumes and sewing equipment out of the building.

'When the show's on, we start to decamp, pack things up, get things down to the next level before all of the other departments wrap,' says Vicky. 'We start the loadout when the show goes live, and when we get to the end of the show, the final items from the quick-change area are packed down and go onto the van.'

Blackpool Memories

Strictly Professional NANCY XU

Nancy Xu grew up in China dreaming of competing in Blackpool, and finally came to England at 17.

'I always explain to people that, if you play basketball, you want to go to the NBA. If you play tennis, you want to get to Wimbledon, and for us, as competitors in Latin and ballroom, especially, the biggest dream for us is to dance in Blackpool,' she says. 'I first danced in Blackpool when I was 17, at the Winter Gardens, which was very special. We'd been watching lots of videos of competitions from there, so to step out on that dance floor, I felt so much emotion. My dream had finally come true. You see the most amazing dancers from around the world and you feel their energy.

'My first ever performance in the Blackpool Tower Ballroom was 2019, which was my first year on *Strictly Come Dancing*. It gave me goose bumps. Then in 2022, I danced there with Will Mellor, which is something I will remember forever. There was so much support from the whole team and everyone's with you. The feeling was amazing.'

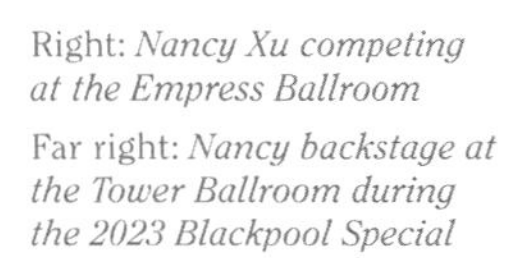

Right: *Nancy Xu competing at the Empress Ballroom*

Far right: *Nancy backstage at the Tower Ballroom during the 2023 Blackpool Special*

Beneath the costume room and beside the girls' dressing room, Lisa Armstrong's make-up team work their magic in another long, narrow room, which is constantly busy with people. Through the back of the room, a door leads to another room, with a small sink, where Lisa Davey's hairstyling team are housed.

'It's quite higgledy-piggledy backstage in Blackpool,' says Lisa Armstrong. 'It's up and down corridors and staircases. We're in the back. But it's just about getting used to a different workspace.'

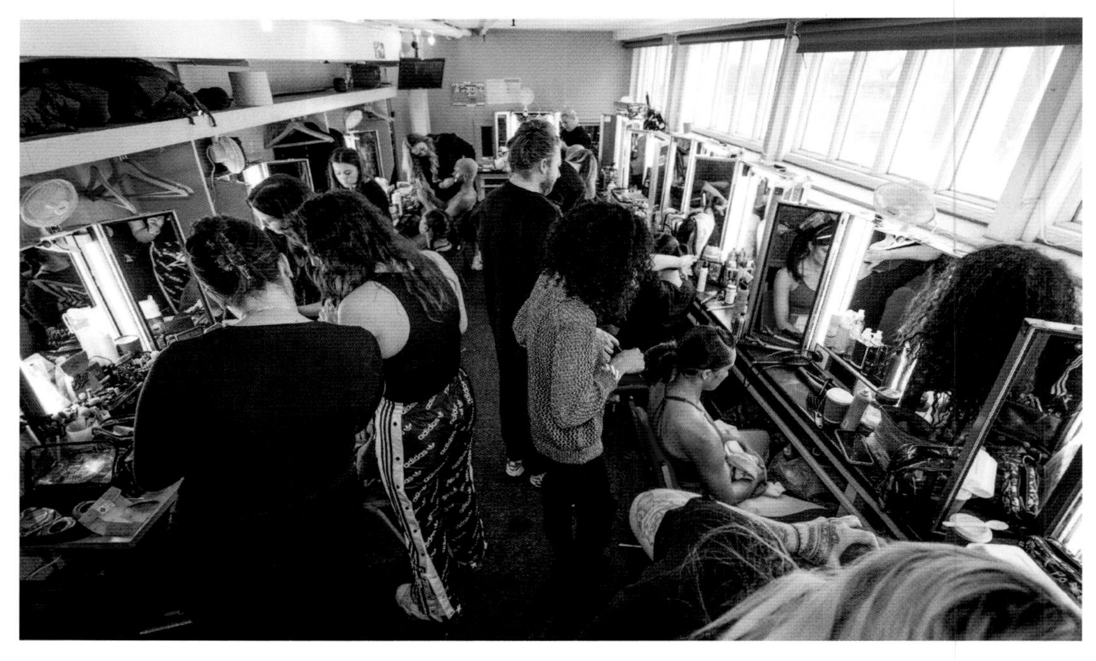

Above: *Views into the busy hair room backstage at the Blackpool Tower*

While the hair room is also narrow, with dryers and tongs heating up the small space, Lisa Davey says it's a popular place for professionals and celebrities to hang out.

'The dancers know where they need to be and they come to us for a bit of downtime. I think they're quite happy to come and sit in a chair and get away from the busy Ballroom,' she says. 'But often, as we do in Elstree, the boys come in to hang out and chat even if they are not having anything done, so it can get pretty busy in that room.'

Above: *Professional dancers Luba Mushtuk and Lauren Oakley relaxing backstage*

In such a huge building, the runners – whose job it is to make sure everyone knows where they need to be and when – have extra yards to cover.

'We've got a larger space to cover at the Tower, so it all takes a bit longer,' says Kate Jones. 'Rather than walking from the gallery straight into the studio, it's quite a way to the OB compound, where the production, sound and lighting gallery trucks are housed, so it requires a lot more people helping out.'

Floor Manager Alan Conley, who needs to make sure each of the professionals and celebrities are in the Ballroom when they are required, says they are not always easy to find. 'At Elstree, the make-up, the wardrobe, the dressing rooms and the Star Bar, where the performers hang out, are next to each other and it's a well-oiled machine,' he says. 'But in Blackpool the rooms are all over the place, so sometimes we have to run around the building trying to find who we need.'

Blackpool Memories

Strictly Professional CARLOS GU

Former Chinese champion Carlos Gu first competed in Blackpool's Winter Gardens at 15.

'Blackpool is just a magical place for all the dancers,' he says. 'When I was 11 or 12 we watched a DVD my teacher brought from England back to China. We had a weekly activity watching Blackpool competitions on the big screen. I was always dreaming that I myself would one day dance there – not winning, but just being there and dancing there. It was like a dream come true for every young kid.

'When I finally got there, at 15, it was my first time in England so I was knocked out by how big it was and also the architecture in the room, so beautiful and such a classic building. I also remember the smell of the floor and the room, which makes you want to dance. You feel every past legend in that room. I was buzzing. My English was terrible so I remember I couldn't talk much, but my dreams had come true.'

Carlos had not been inside the Tower Ballroom before 2022, his first year on *Strictly Come Dancing*, when he danced with Molly Rainford. 'I like the Tower Ballroom better than the Winter Gardens nowadays because it's more intimate, it's darker and feeds your imagination, with the dance floor and all the red and gold interior design. Everything was so beautifully designed and I really love the smell of old buildings and of the wood floor. It makes you feel like you're dancing without moving.

'Blackpool is a milestone on the *Strictly* journey, and if you get to Blackpool you have done something amazing for yourself and your partner. I have now danced there with Molly and with Angela Scanlon in 2023, where we did the Argentine Tango and scored three 10s, which was amazing.'

Left: *Carlos Gu and Angela Scanlon dancing the Argentine Tango during the 2023 Blackpool Special*

CHAPTER

9

Blackpool Memories

For young Latin and ballroom dancers, competing in Blackpool is a dream come true. Since 1920, the Empress Ballroom in the Winter Gardens has hosted the Blackpool Dance Festival every May. The 14-day festival is comprised of 13 different events, and includes the British Open Championships, one of the most prestigious contests for adult amateur and professional couples and formation teams.

The Blackpool Junior Dance Festival, which began in 1957, is held at Easter and took place in the Tower Ballroom until 2010, when it moved to the Winter Gardens. The seven-day event incorporates the British Junior and Juvenile Open Championships, for 6 to under-12s and 12 to under-16s respectively. In total there are 38 competitions across three disciplines of Latin, Ballroom and Sequence. The *Strictly Come Dancing* Blackpool weekend typically coincides with the British National Dance Championship, which take place at the Empress Ballroom. The three-day event includes adult, juvenile and junior dancers in ballroom and Latin. *Strictly Come Dancing* professionals and judges are among those who have happy memories of the spiritual home of ballroom, having competed there as children and adults.

Judge Anton Du Beke competed at the Winter Gardens with Erin Boag from 1997 to 2002.

'During our competitive career, the Blackpool Dance Festival in May was the highlight of the calendar,' he says. 'Just being up there and being part of it for the week was an incredible feeling. It felt like the climax of the year. I had good results and I had bad results, but it was always an amazing week of incredible dancing.

'I've been coming to Blackpool with *Strictly Come Dancing* since 2004 and it is a brilliant week in the series. There's an incredible energy, and because it's not in a television studio but in the Tower Ballroom in Blackpool, there's a whole different vibe. You've got a wonderful crowd, the biggest of the series, and it's an extraordinary feeling.

'For Blackpool, I always tried to have something ballroom, like an American Smooth or Quickstep, that would move around the floor or that has a lift. I had one of my best nights on *Strictly* in Blackpool when I got two 10s for the American Smooth with Emma Barton in 2019.'

Left: *Anton Du Beke and Emma Barton performing the American Smooth during the 2019 Blackpool Special*

Amy Dowden started competing at Blackpool at the age of eight, in a formation team, and won the World Championship at the Winter Gardens, with now-husband Ben, in 2016.

'We'd been to Disney World a few months before my first trip to Blackpool,' she says. 'But I walked into the Tower Ballroom and I turned to my mum and said, "This is better than Disney World." They had to bribe me to leave the front row that day. It was the World Formation Latin Championships for the under-12s and under-16s, so there were couples from America, China, Russia, Ukraine, you name it, and I was just mesmerised. There was one particular dancer that I loved in the under-16s – and it was Kevin Clifton! I wanted to be just like him. That day, I told my mum I wanted to be a professional dancer, but it also made me determined to get a boy partner, because I'd been dancing with my twin sister. For weeks afterwards, I asked my dance teacher, "Have you got me one of those boys yet?" So even at eight years old, I knew I wanted to be a professional dancer and I wanted to win at Blackpool.

'I was lucky enough to be crowned British National Champion in 2016, on 19 November. Then six years on, to the day, I led the group number on *Strictly* at Blackpool with junior dancer Pebble-Rose Spratt playing little Amy, walking into that Ballroom and having those dreams. It was a real pinch-me moment. Imagine telling my younger self that she could win at Blackpool and dance on *Strictly*, all those years later. It was like coming full circle and that dance meant so much to me. I'm grateful to *Strictly* for giving me that opportunity.'

Below left: *Amy Dowden competing at the Tower Ballroom as a child*
Below right: *Pebble-Rose Spratt playing a younger version of Amy during a performance at the 2022 Blackpool Special*

Above: *Jason Gilkison and his dance partner winning the Amateur Latin championships in Blackpool, 1989*

Jason Gilkison, *Strictly*'s Creative Director, danced with partner Peta Roby from the age of seven and they were undefeated Australian Champions from 1981 to 1997. They also bagged three Blackpool crowns, winning the Youth Competition in 1985, the Amateur Latin Championship in 1989 and the Professional Rising Stars award in 1990.

'My grandfather, Sam Gilkison, was a pioneer in the ballroom dancing world and opened the first dance studio in Perth, Australia, in 1931. But he was born and raised in Scotland and was trained in the UK, in some of the best dance studios in London. He used to tell me stories about hitchhiking down from Scotland, with a mate, to go to dances at the Tower Ballroom every weekend. I remember listening to his stories about the place when I was a child, and I finally went there to compete all those years later, and then became World Champion at the Amateur Latin Championship there, in 1989.

'My first visit from Australia was in 1983 and we were really lucky to get into the Amateur Latin final at the Dance Festival . We'd had three weeks' training in London and then everybody says, "We're going up to Blackpool." Coming from Australia, I had no idea what Blackpool meant, but I remember walking into the Tower Ballroom for the first time and it was exactly as I'd imagined from my grandfather's description. You never forget your first step into that ballroom. At first you want to back out and run away because it's so overwhelming. It was such a weird and emotional feeling walking down the stairs, and it felt like coming full circle for me.

'Coming down the Promenade, from our hotel, Blackpool Tower gets bigger and bigger as you're driving towards it, and it brings back so many memories of what it was like to dance there. All my highlights, the biggest moments of my dance career as a competitor, were at Blackpool.'

Neil Jones and Katya Jones first met in Blackpool in 2008 and went on to form a winning partnership, being crowned Amateur Latin Champions at the 2012 Blackpool Dance Festival. They also became undefeated four-time British National Champions, and the three-time World Amateur Latin Champions. Katya's first experience of the Tower Ballroom was in the Blackpool Junior Dance Festival, at 13, and she danced at the Winter Gardens every year from 2006 until turning professional in 2013.

'I was born and raised in Russia, and we all knew that to come to Blackpool you have to be good enough to compete,' she says. 'When we arrived in Blackpool and came to the Tower, it was very special because we knew the history, how many championships have happened here and how prestigious it is. We loved the grandness of it.

'We used to go on the dinosaur ride in between the rounds. It was an incredible experience for all these kids from around the world, thinking, "Wow, I've made it." Just going abroad was a big deal, let alone entering a gorgeous ballroom like the Tower.

'The first time I came to compete here as a teenager, I was dancing alongside Oti Mabuse. Years later, in 2016, when I saw her on *Strictly*, it all clicked together, and I said, "Oh my goodness. We used to compete together."

'We all get excited about coming to Blackpool, but it's not until you're actually there that you remember how cool it is.'

Above: *Neil Jones and Katya Jones as children, wearing dance costumes*

Neil Jones began competing in Blackpool at the age of nine and would dance at both the Winter Gardens and the Tower Ballroom on numerous occasions throughout his amateur career.

'Blackpool was where it all started for me,' Neil says. 'When I was younger, we danced in medallist competitions (where solo children can dance with their teacher and are judged singly) and in my first year I was ranked the number-two boy in the whole country. That was my first taste of being in a final and doing well and I wanted more. The first time I danced in the Tower Ballroom was for the junior World Open Championships, when I was 13. I remember watching dancers from the top countries in the world, such as Iceland, Ukraine and Russia, and thinking, "I want to be as good as all of them." It was those special moments that drove me to dance and win competitions.

'As kids, we would run to Jungle Jim's adventure play area in the Blackpool Tower between rounds and play on all the soft toys. Our parents would come running after us, saying, "Get back in, you're on in 10 minutes." That was so much fun. Even now, when I walk in and smell the building, it brings back so many memories.'

Ukrainian professional Nadiya Bychkova is a former Slovenian Ballroom and Latin Champion and two-time World and European Champion.

'My first ever competition in England was in the Tower Ballroom when I was 10 years old. There were five couples, coming all the way from Ukraine, and I remember looking forward to it. It was a big adventure as a child and I made the final in the under-16s, so it was a successful first Blackpool experience.'

Above: *Nadiya Bychkova during a visit to Blackpool as a young dancer*

Left: *Kai Widdrington and Nadiya Bychkova dancing at the Tower Ballroom during the 2022 Blackpool Special*

Kai Widdrington entered his debut competition at the age of eight, a year after watching the first series of *Strictly* inspired him to take to the dance floor.

'I remember holding my grandma's hand and walking down the steps to get into the Tower Ballroom. Hearing the iconic orchestra, seeing the wooden dance floor and watching these beautiful silhouettes of ballroom dancers glide, it didn't seem real. My dad always drove me to Blackpool from Southampton, which was a five- or six-hour journey. My family would always come ... it is a fond memory. We would stay in a little B&B and do the amusement arcades.'

Kai also recalls a moment when his grandmother's homemade sandwiches almost cost him his career. It was time to take to the dance floor, but Kai was still busy eating. 'The music starts and I have this tuna sandwich and I'm doing the Samba with cheeks puffed out.

'Walking into the Blackpool Ballroom was like walking into another world of ballroom dancing, seeing all the guys dressed in tail suits and the girls in the beautiful ballroom dresses. If you fall in love with dancing like I did, you fall in love with Blackpool. There's nothing but happy memories there.'

Graziano Di Prima didn't compete in Blackpool as a child and first stood on the hallowed dance floor at the Tower Ballroom when he joined *Strictly* in 2018.

'The first time was magical,' he says. 'Giovanni and I led an Italian group number, set in the 1950s, when we were love rivals fighting over a girl, and it was great fun. The love that place and that audience gives you is incredible. It feels almost like you are in an arena, but it is so beautiful, and because the audience is above you, and all around, it's a different sound. You can feel that energy flow towards you. You feel part of history.

'I danced the Paso Doble there with Kym Marsh in 2022 and that was incredible. Blackpool is one of the most wonderful weeks on *Strictly*. It's close to the Final and it's one of the big goals, as a professional, you want to achieve.'

Right: *Graziano Di Prima and his childhood dance partner*

Below: *The professional dancers' routine at the results show for the Blackpool Special, 2018*

Lauren Oakley began competing at seven and won the Juvenile Open Championship across both ballroom and Latin disciplines at the Blackpool Junior Dance Festival. She was also the under-21 British National Champion in 2008.

'My mum danced in Blackpool when she was pregnant with me, my cousin has danced there, and I competed in Blackpool three times a year, every year, from the age of seven, so it has been in the family for a while,' she says. 'I don't remember ever spending an Easter which wasn't at Blackpool. We used to have Easter-egg hunts in the arcades.

'Being there with *Strictly* is like going home. It's just got this magical air about it because of all the ballroom and Latin legends that have danced there. Even if you go there and the music isn't playing, you can hear it in your head and it's lovely.'

Gorka Márquez first danced in Blackpool after joining Strictly in 2016 and has partnered Alexandra Burke and Helen Skelton at the Tower Ballroom.

'Blackpool is like the Wimbledon of dance,' he says. 'Growing up I always wanted to compete there, but I never had the chance. The first time I danced in the Tower, with *Strictly*, what amazed me most was the dance floor. The whole Ballroom was bouncing with us.

'I danced the Quickstep there with both Alexandra Burke in 2017 and Helen Skelton in 2022 and got 39 each time. For Helen, Blackpool was a turning point. It built her confidence and was a joyful moment, when she thought, "I can do this." That was when you could see her personality, the cheeky, funny person that she is away from the cameras, for the first time. It was a beautiful dance.'

Top: *Lauren Oakley performing on* Strictly Come Dancing *in 2022*
Bottom: *Gorka Márquez dancing as a small child*
Right: *Gorka Márquez and Helen Skelton dancing the Quickstep in the 2022 Blackpool Special*

Above: *Nikita Kuzmin and Layton Williams dancing their Couple's Choice in the 2023 Blackpool Special*
Right: *Nikita sharing a friendly moment backstage at the Tower ballroom*

Six-time Italian Champion Nikita Kuzmin competed at the Tower Ballroom for the first time when he was eight – and it didn't quite go to plan.

'Blackpool was the competition that I was most scared of, and I remember coming onto the dance floor at the Tower Ballroom for the first time when I was eight,' he says. 'To cut a long story short, I was so nervous I danced in the wrong heat for all the dances. My parents couldn't stop me because I was already on the floor, doing the wrong thing at the wrong time. I was eliminated in the first round!

'I have so many memories from Blackpool – it's like a winter wonderland for dancers, especially for kids. You come inside and your eyes start to shine. Just being there, going up the Tower and seeing the whole of the city is amazing. Performing there with Layton Williams, in 2023, was one of my *Strictly* highlights. To come back with the show every year, and dancing on that famous dance floor, I still get that adrenaline rush.'

CHAPTER

10

10
10
10

When Blackpool Rocks

Strictly Come Dancing first came to Blackpool in 2004, and the Tower Ballroom has been home to some of the show's most iconic moments. From routines that broke previous records or bagged a perfect score to those memorable dances that entered the annals of history for sheer entertainment value, here's a look at the some of the many showstoppers performed on the famous dance floor.

Above: *Dianne Buswell and Joe Sugg performing the Quickstep in the 2018 Blackpool Special*

Blackpool Memories

Strictly Professional DIANNE BUSWELL

Growing up in Australia, where she was national Open Champion, Dianne Buswell never got the chance to compete in Blackpool. But since joining *Strictly* she has partnered Joe Sugg and Tyler West at the Tower.

'I think my favourite memory of Blackpool was dancing the Quickstep with Joe Sugg in 2018 and receiving three 10s. It was so magical. It made the little Dianne in me feel like she had made it. It was so special. After all those years of wanting to compete there, it all came true, and I admit I shed a little tear.'

Right: *Natasha Kaplinsky and Brendan Cole dancing at the Tower Ballroom in 2004*

Tower Trailblazers

The first ever series of the show, in the spring of 2004, moved to the Tower Ballroom in week three with Verona Joseph, Lesley Garrett, Martin Offiah, David Dickinson, Christopher Parker, Claire Sweeney and Natasha Kaplinsky all taking to the dance floor. Claire topped the leaderboard on the night, scoring 34 for her Tango, to The Police's hit 'Roxanne'. Natasha, who went on to become the first *Strictly* champion, narrowly avoided elimination after landing in the bottom two, but David bowed out.

Above: *Erin Boag and Martin Offiah dancing at the Tower Ballroom in 2004*

Left: *Members of the camera crew setting up for the first* Strictly Come Dancing *show to be broadcast from Blackpool*

Above: *Darren Bennett and Jill Halfpenny performing the Jive in the Blackpool Special, autumn 2004*

The Grand Final

Series two, in the autumn of the same year as the first-ever series, treated viewers to two trips to Blackpool, with a mid-series special and a return, three weeks later, for the Grand Final. On both outings, former *EastEnders* star Jill Halfpenny came out top – scoring 38 for her week-five Samba before lifting the Glitterball trophy in the Tower Ballroom with partner Darren Bennett. As three couples battled it out in the spectacular Final, Jill performed her iconic Jive, appropriately to Elton John's 'I'm Still Standing', and landed the show's first ever perfect score of 40.

A Waltz to Remember

The show returned to Blackpool in 2009 with nine couples heading north in week eight. Ali Bastian and partner Brian Fortuna stole the show with a beautiful Viennese Waltz, to 'Do Right Woman, Do Right Man' by Etta James, scoring a perfect 40. Bringing out his dusty 10 paddle, Craig Revel Horwood joked: 'I'm very disappointed. I could not find a single thing wrong with it.'

Right: *Brian Fortuna and Ali Bastian dancing the Viennese Waltz in the 2009 Blackpool Special*

Below: *The judges deliver their verdict on the stunning waltz – a perfect score*

Strictly *History*

Series eight in 2010 saw Matt Di Angelo top the Blackpool leaderboard with his Samba, earning an impressive 38 points. But perhaps the most iconic dance from the show was Anton Du Beke's Samba with Ann Widdecombe, to 'Heaven Must Be Missing an Angel' by Tavares. The former Conservative MP, dressed in canary yellow, was spun round on the floor by her professional partner in a move that went down in *Strictly* history. Former judge Len Goodman commented: 'I've learned the secret of crop circles. You must have been practising in a cornfield.'

Left: *Pasha Kovalev and Chelsee Healey dancing their Show Dance in the 2011 Final*

Below: *Kristina Rihanoff and Jason Donovan dancing their Show Dance in the 2011 Final*

All About Harry

The only other Grand Final beamed from the Ballroom besides series two took place in 2011, when Harry Judd took the crown after a close-run Final against Jason Donovan and Chelsee Healey. Not one judge scored lower than nine and, while Jason scored top marks for his showstopping showdance, Harry and partner Aliona Vilani pipped their competitors to the post by landing two perfect scores for their Quickstep and their Argentine Tango.

Left: *Anton Du Beke and Ann Widdecombe dancing the Samba in the 2010 Blackpool Special*

Right: *2011 winners Harry Judd and Aliona Vilani*

Above: *Oti Mabuse and Danny Mac dancing the Charleston in the 2016 Blackpool Special*
Below: *Ed Balls descending from the roof of the Tower Ballroom in front of a blazing piano*

Ritzy Routine

Danny Mac and partner Oti Mabuse were awarded the first 40 of the series in 2016, when they raised the roof in the Tower Ballroom with a Charleston to 'Puttin' on the Ritz' by Gregory Porter. Former judge Bruno Tonioli called it a 'table-topping showstopper' and Craig Revel Horwood commented: 'One word, three syllables, darling: FAB-U-LOUS.' The same year saw another iconic routine, with former shadow Chancellor of the Exchequer Ed Balls descending from the roof playing a piano, for his 'Great Balls of Fire' Jive with Katya Jones, as flames shot into the air. The live track ended with a lyric change to 'Goodness gracious, Ed Balls of fire' and, while the score of 23 failed to set the leaderboard alight, viewers thought the entertaining number was scorching hot.

Below: *Pasha Kovalev and Ashley Roberts dancing the Jive in the 2018 Blackpool Special*

Shake It Up

Former Pussycat Doll Ashley Roberts Jived her way into the *Strictly* history books with a Blackpool Jive in 2018, to 'Shake Your Tail Feather' by the Blues Brothers, which Shirley Ballas said had 'pushed the envelope'. Ashley and her professional partner Pasha Kovalev were handed the first top marks of the series.

Blackpool Memories

Former *Strictly* Champion JOWITA PRZYSTAŁ

Jowita Przystał had not set foot in the Tower Ballroom before she made her debut as a professional dancer on the show with Hamza Yassin in series 20. The pair scored 38 for their American Smooth, to Frank Sinatra's 'New York, New York' and went on to win the series.

'My first time in Blackpool was in 2022, when Hamza and I opened the show. I still have goose bumps if I think about it. It was very special to me. Even entering the Ballroom made me feel emotional. There's something you can't describe about that place. I think it's the atmosphere. You just need to be there and feel that energy. It's purely magical.'

Below: *Jowita Przystal and Hamza Yassin dancing the American Smooth in the 2022 Blackpool Special*

Right: *Vito Coppola and Fleur East dancing their Couple's Choice in the 2022 Blackpool Special*

Blackpool Memories

Strictly Professional VITO COPPOLA

Vito Coppola followed his iconic Blackpool debut with Fleur East in 2022 by topping the leaderboard in his second year as a professional on the show, with a score of 39 for a fabulous Charleston with Ellie Leach. But the Tower Ballroom also holds one very happy childhood memory for the Italian dancer.

'Blackpool is my favourite place,' he says. 'It is where the most important competitions in the world take place, so for a dancer it's gold. I competed in the Tower Ballroom and I won the junior competition when I was 15, in 2007, which was amazing. It was at Easter, and I remember I wanted to reach the highest point of the Tower, so we went up to where the glass floor is under your feet and I walked across it. That kind of memory stays with you for life.

'Walking into the Ballroom, you can feel the energy, the vibe, the atmosphere, the history and the many champions who have stepped on that same dance floor before you. It's incredible to think I was dancing on the same dance floor as the idols I'd been watching for years before I was able to come here. That history, the background, the past gives you a buzz.

'The next time I went to Blackpool was in 2022 with Fleur East and we had our first perfect score of the series, with the Couple's Choice dance to the Destiny's Child medley, and it was epic. I had the best time. Also dancing the Charleston with Ellie Leach in 2023 was amazing. Every single time I go to Blackpool there's a good feeling and it's so memorable – and not just because I got good results! I just love Blackpool. It brings me good energy.'

Left: *Giovanni Pernice and Georgia May Foote dancing the Foxtrot in the 2015 Blackpool Special*

Blackpool Memories

Strictly Professional GIOVANNI PERNICE

Giovanni Pernice has danced on the Ballroom dance floor with celebrity partners Faye Tozer in 2018, Debbie McGee in 2017 and Georgia May Foote in 2015, who scored an impressive 38 for her American Smooth.

'It's a real achievement for the celebrity to get there,' he says. 'Everybody gets excited when we go to Blackpool because we are going on a trip with all the cast and crew. Also, the place itself is just unbelievable. I never performed in Blackpool when I was a kid, so, for me, the first time entering the Ballroom was sensational. I saw this incredible place – the chandeliers are huge! For a dancer, the sprung dance floor is amazing as well. The Ballroom is scintillating, remarkable, a beautiful place.'

Blackpool Memories

Strictly Professional JOHANNES RADEBE

South African Latin champion Johannes Radebe first performed at the Tower Ballroom with *Strictly*, and in 2023 he partnered Annabel Croft in a moving American Smooth.

'As a dancer, I knew about Blackpool before I knew about London,' he says. 'But *Strictly Come Dancing* in 2018 was my first time at the Tower Ballroom. I didn't have a celebrity partner so I was in the group numbers – including a magical opener with Gloria Estefan. A real pinch-me moment! The Ballroom has the perfect dance floor and means everyone dances their best. It's such an iconic place to dance and it was beautiful to see it through Annabel Croft's eyes. I'm so grateful to *Strictly* for giving me the chance to dance in Blackpool.'

Above: *Johannes Radebe and Annabel Croft dancing the American Smooth in the 2023 Blackpool Special*

AUTHOR'S ACKNOWLEDGEMENTS

With many thanks to Blackpool Council, the team at *Strictly Come Dancing*, Michael Williams, Managing Director of the Winter Gardens Marina Blore from Fit The Bill, Samantha Bell-Docherty and Aishley Bell-Docherty, House of Wingz and the team at the Showtown Museum.

With special thanks to Kate Shane and her colleagues at Blackpool Tower, who were generous with their time, resources and extensive knowledge.

PICTURE CREDITS:

Guy Levy pp. 4, 8, 10, 10, 20–23, 28–31, 52, 76 (top left), 92–97, 101–116, 119–121, 128–139,148–149, 154–159, 162–189, 205, 222–224; Guy Levy/BBC pp. 68, 81, 91, 98, 117, 122, 124, 142–147, 151, 160, 190, 196, 197 (right), 200 (left), 201 (bottom), 202 (top), 203, 204, 208, 210, 213,–221; BBC Photo Archive (pp.9, 35, 71 and 212); Getty (p.41 WPA Pool (bottom right); pp.54, 60, 62 and 75 Christopher Furlong; 84 Hulton Deutsch); Showtown Blackpool (pp.11–18, 24–27, 34, 36, 38–40, 41 (bottom left), 42–44, 46–48, 69–70, 72–74, 76 (bottom), 77–78, 82–83, 85–87); Phil Kelsall (p.37); Jason Lock (p.45); Kate Shane (pp. 56–59, 64); Ross Morgan (p.63); The Dame Gracie Fields Appreciation Society (p.80); Nancy Xu (p.186); Alamy (p.194 Billy Stock); Amy Dowden (p.197, left); Neil Jones (p.199, left); Katya Jones (p.199, right); Nadiya Bychkova (p.200, top); Graziano Di Prima (p.201, top); Gorka Márquez (p.202, bottom); Abi Wyles/BBC (p.211); Blackpool Tower Illustration: AdobeStock